Heartfelt

TEACHERS ARE PEOPLE TOO

Robert U. Montgomery

RUM PUBLISHING

Heartfelt
Teachers Are People Too
Robert U. Montgomery
RUM Publishing

Published by RUM Publishing, Bonne Terre, MO
Copyright ©2022 Robert U. Montgomery
All rights reserved.

No part of this publication may be reproduced, stored in a retrieval system, or transmitted in any form or by any means, electronic, mechanical, photocopying, recording, scanning, or otherwise, except as permitted under Section 107 or 108 of the 1976 United States Copyright Act, without the prior written permission of the Publisher. Requests to the Publisher for permission should be addressed to Permissions Department, RUM Publishing, roticomontgomery@gmail.com

Names, characters, businesses, places, events and incidents are either the products of the author's imagination or used in a fictitious manner. Any resemblance to actual persons, living or dead, or actual events is purely coincidental.

Project Management and Book Design:
 DavisCreativePublishingPartners.com

Publisher's Cataloging-In-Publication Data

ISBNB: 978-1-7330033-7-7

LCCN: 2022916392

1. BIO026000   BIOGRAPHY & AUTOBIOGRAPHY / Personal Memoirs
    2. TRV001000   TRAVEL / Special Interest / Adventure
    3. EDU029000   EDUCATION / Teaching / General

ATTENTION CORPORATIONS, UNIVERSITIES, COLLEGES AND PROFESSIONAL ORGANIZATIONS: Quantity discounts are available on bulk purchases of this book for educational, gift purposes, or as premiums for increasing magazine subscriptions or renewals. Special books or book excerpts can also be created to fit specific needs. For information, please contact Robert U. Montgomery, RUM Publishing, roticomontgomery@gmail.com, http://rumpublishing.com.

*This book is dedicated to
the memory of my good friend
and fellow teacher,
Shirley Jovanovic,
a sweet soul who died much too young.
She is the woman in the cover photo,
enjoying a winter sunset on
an isolated Florida beach.*

Table of Contents

Introduction 1

I: Virgin 3

II: Veteran 79

III: Heartfelt 167

IV: Loss 193

V: Discovery 223

About the Author. 265

Introduction

Rarely have I allowed practicality to influence a life-altering decision. I lead with my heart.

But the single notable time I followed practicality led to one of the most painful emotional experiences of my life. It followed hard on the heels of a relationship where I blindly followed my heart and suffered even more. You can read about both in this story.

Nearly forty years later, I still feel the same way about those events, I realized, as I transcribed journal entries from that time into book form. I also learned that too often I was a jerk with women, probably because I was afraid of allowing myself to be vulnerable. Is that typical male behavior or was I the exception? Don't ask me.

My heart also led me into teaching, following a brief newspaper career, a failed marriage, and an adventure in Europe. This book also is about my foray into that profession, as a high school journalism and English teacher. Following my heart there definitely was the right choice for me. I loved teaching. I loved the students. They were my "kids."

A principal once told me that it must be nice to not need the money, since I often forgot to pick up my paycheck. That was not the case. I needed money to pay bills. But I simply didn't associate what I loved to do with being paid for it.

This book is about my first three years of teaching at two different schools, my search for companionship and romance, family conflict, tragic loss, and recovery, punctuated by an adventure in Africa, all told in journal entries at the time events occurred.

If you are a teacher or retired teacher, especially at the high school level, I think you will identify with much of what I experienced in the classroom. If you are a woman looking to better understand men, I think you will find my observations mostly entertaining but maybe even helpful. And if you are a man, I suspect you will shake your head in disbelief at my romantic ineptness, especially regarding a certain flight attendant.

Author's note: This is a sequel to My Neighbor Was a Serial Killer: A Writer's Memories of Mayhem, Romance, and Murder. *It features some of the same people. But reading the first book is not a prerequisite for enjoying the second.*

I: Virgin

1981

Monday, August 31, Webster Groves, Missouri

Today was my first as a teacher. All day I felt as if I'd shatter and fall to pieces if I relaxed for moment. So I kept moving.

There's something about the newness that makes me feel terribly inadequate. Maybe it's the anonymity. No one there really knows me. And, as yet, no one really cares. Without someone caring or recognizing my worth, I guess I feel I'm a nonperson.

The students were all right. I've been told the first few days are a "honeymoon" period and no one misbehaves.

The heat and humidity were horrible. That made the day seem longer, I think. Movement was an effort. I came home exhausted.

Part of my tiredness, though, was due to not sleeping last night. That was because of a combination of factors. First, I played softball all day Sunday, as we finished second in a tournament, and I still was keyed up from that. Second, I was nervous about my first day.

And then I was nervous about being nervous and not being able to sleep. During the little time I did sleep, I dreamed I was walking around in my softball uniform, trying to find a place to sleep.

The choir director across the hall from my room seems like a person I'd like to know better. She has a quick laugh and beautiful eyes.

Jerry Knight, the principal, continues to impress me. He's open, honest, and easygoing. But he's not easygoing because he's lazy. He's that way because he sees that is the way to accomplish the most. Also, he doesn't let himself or others get bogged down with inconsequential things that have little or nothing to do with providing students with a good education.

Wednesday, September 2

I'm gaining confidence at school. But I've a long way to go. Each class period still seems forever. And, at the same time, it seems as if I hurry through everything I talk about.

Last year's adviser for the *Echo*, who is on maternity leave, told me that it was impossible to find someone who would produce the school newspaper for less than she was paying to a company called Messenger. Because of what she said, I was reluctant to try. But then I saw a weekly publication called the *Webster-Kirkwood Times*.

I was impressed by its looks and its writing. Because of the good feeling I got from that paper, I decided to investigate the possibility of it handling our paper's production. So now it appears the *Times* will do the work for far less than the old company, $380 compared to $555, and we'll get two hundred and fifty more copies of each issue.

The paper is $1,000 in the red right now, and this savings will help immensely.

The editors, John and Carl, seem to like the idea of changing. Although this was my idea and I'm in favor of it too, I'm still a little scared. Messenger handled the school paper for a long time. This is a big step for a new teacher, and all eyes, I'm certain, are watching.

The old adviser also told me I wouldn't be able to get the *St. Louis Post-Dispatch* newspaper for my journalism students to read. She was wrong there too.

Why, I wonder, did she discourage me from trying to do these things?

*****

The journalism students nearly all seem to come from upper-middle class homes. I had them write about themselves. Their lives are in decided contrast to the students I had while substituting at Central High School in Flat River. Also, most of them seem polite, well mannered, and respectful. But it remains to be seen whether I will hold that same opinion in a month.

I think I should explain that contrast. Based on what they wrote, these kids have wealth. They have weekend homes on lakes. They have show horses. They dress well. Their fathers are executives. Their mothers are artists or volunteer workers.

There don't seem to be as many broken homes, as many alcoholics, or as many cases of child abuse as there are in communities like Flat River.

Or maybe these kids just don't talk or write about it.

Tuesday, September 8

This is the story of an old, ugly, blue baseball cap. Before I moved up here, I threw it away. The next day, there it was back on the cow-horns hat rack in the bedroom at my parents' house.

I didn't have to ask who pulled it out of the trash and put it back. I knew. My mother.

Someone else might have rescued it and brought it to me, asking if I meant to throw it away. Not my mother. It didn't matter to her whether I meant to throw it away. She wasn't going to let me. She said nothing to me. I said nothing to her.

When I got ready to move some things up here, I stashed the cap in the bottom of my knapsack, intending to throw it away when I got up here. Then I forgot about it.

Back at Flat River the next weekend, I saw the cap behind my mother's chair in the living room. This past weekend, it was back on the hat rack. I smuggled it back up here, and it is now in my kitchen trash. At least I think it is in my kitchen trash.

Yeah, I realize that some will think I'm cruel for the way I handled this, and they might be correct. But here's the thing: all Mom had to do was tell me that she wanted to keep the cap for nostalgic reasons or whatever. Instead, she played this passive-aggressive game that she so often does.

And yeah, I played it right back. I'm not proud of it.

*****

The first paper is scheduled to come out September 24. Some of the other teachers have their doubts, or at least they seem to want to give that impression, I think. Carl, one of the editors, said he thought that too. Why they would want to or expect us to fail, I don't know. And I know too little right now to even hazard an educated guess.

Of course, I have my doubts too. We have only a little more than two weeks and we're barely started. What will happen? Stay tuned.

I'm still getting along well with the kids. And the classes are passing more quickly.

The amount of paperwork still is nearly staggering. But I'm managing—I think.

Right now, my schedule is school, home to sleep, and back to school. I have to enrich it some way.

Tuesday, September 15

My cartoonist is an award winner, I'm told. He also is bizarre. He looks like a cartoon character, with his long face, curly hair, and glasses. And he delights in trying to sneak in obscene words and gestures, as well as other little surprises, into his work. His first two submissions contained a middle finger and a minister named Fartwell. Dealing with this guy should be lots of fun.

We sent our copy to the typesetter today. Layout will start Thursday. E-Day grows closer and closer.

I gave my first test in journalism class today. The most depressing part was the spelling words, words I had taken from the students' papers. Most of them cannot spell "naïve" (nieve) or "yacht" (yaught), and those are only two small examples.

But some students in each of the three classes seem interested and do seem to try their best. The make the work worthwhile.

Monday, September 21

I'm very tired. We worked until seven p.m. on the *Echo*. Actually, John and Carl did most of the work. I supervised and occasionally assisted. They did a good job, especially for the first time.

Tomorrow we paste on the corrections and headlines and then take the paper to the printer. We plan to sell it at school on Thursday. So far, no major catastrophes.

But the paper is not out yet.

Mike, the bizarre cartoonist, brought in his work at the last minute. We couldn't find any hidden obscenities in his attack upon capitalism, the draft, national defense, and the Moral Majority. I pray no one else will be able to either.

*****

The principal sat in on one of my journalism classes Wednesday. He gave me a really good evaluation report, which was a great relief. I know I'm good, but I was afraid someone else might not recognize the fact so readily. Yeah, that's sarcasm.

I do know that I'm a better teacher with second and third period than with first. I'm not sure why. But practice, I imagine, has a lot to do with it. Also, maybe the kids aren't yet awake during first hour and so aren't very responsive.

That being said, I also enjoy second and third more than first.

*****

Our coed softball team won the league tournament this past weekend. We had to play five games on Saturday to do it. I ran into the outfield fence trying to catch a fly ball in the championship game. I bruised my left arm, stretched a couple of leg muscles, and banged my ribs pretty good. In short, I'm a walking sore.

My teammates now call me "Mad Dog."

*****

So far, I've gone home to Flat River every weekend. I'm going to stop doing that soon.

Thursday, September 24

Our first paper was distributed today. Reaction was good—at least it seemed that way. I, too, was pleased, although we made many careless mistakes in the paste-up process. But I expected those kinds of errors. No one on the staff had ever done that type of work before. Previous printer took care of paste-up, which is why it charged more.

The writing was good in general, and so were the photos.

One of the teachers said he could tell by looking at the paper that the person in charge had real newspaper experience. I really didn't do that much. The students did most all the work. I helped only when a problem arose.

*****

I talked to my friend Robbie in New York City tonight. He said he just produced a program for CBS. Also, he's had some success selling magazine articles.

He and Karen broke up, which is not surprising since they've been separated by half a continent for two years. She's in Kansas City, where they met when he worked for a radio station there.

Wednesday, September 30

We got paid today. Finally! After paying bills and buying food, I have $60 left for October.

*****

I staged a confrontation in my journalism classes today with the help of two drama students. They barged in, interrupting class and complaining about the paper's coverage of the school musical. Soon, they were yelling at me and I was yelling back.

One of them called me a "twerp," and then they stormed out. I threw a book at them, then ran out into the hall and yelled one more time.

Our first performance was a little rough—too much smiling, mostly by me. But things went well the other two hours.

Most of the students were genuinely startled. When I came back in and smiled, third hour applauded.

All of this was done as an exercise in observation. Students wrote about what they saw and heard. A few criticized my acting. The rats!

*****

Slowly but surely, I'm adjusting to living up here in a duplex, as I also relax more and enjoy my time at school. I'm feeling a lot better and not nearly as tired as I was. I'm staying up here this weekend—for the first time.

Sunday, October 4

I've been sick all day. I can't keep anything down. I sure hope I don't have to miss school tomorrow. I'm guessing the problem might be something I ate last night at the Mexican restaurant.

My mother didn't have such a good time either. She started choking and couldn't stop. Craig grasped her around the middle and pressed in hard.

She kept struggling. But on my brother's third try, whatever had been choking her became dislodged and she could breathe again.

Restaurant employees acted quickly, calling paramedics within seconds of when she started choking, and several of them came to make certain she was all right.

When Mom started choking, I didn't do anything but ask Craig if he knew the life-saving technique. I figured he did, since he works at a hospital. If he hadn't, I could have. I'm glad I didn't have to. And I'm glad he was able to do something so heroic.

He said later he felt as if he were panicking. But he didn't seem that way to me. He seemed pretty calm.

As usual, my father couldn't express real concern or sympathy, even if he felt it. My mother almost died, and he was trying to make light of it only a few minutes later, talking about how he would have put her on the floor and "squashed her like a duck" to keep her from choking.

Tuesday, October 13

Yesterday was my birthday. I'm thirty-three. How and when did I become so old?

I spent twelve hours of that day at school, teaching and then supervising paste-up for the paper. Our second issue comes out Thursday, and Monday was the day when we had to do most of the production work. I think this one is going to look a lot more professional than our first.

Now that we've had two papers and I have something to base my assessments on, I'm going to have individual conferences with staff members to discuss their work.

We have eighteen, and the most difficult assignment for me seems to be keeping everyone busy. But I'm getting there. John and Carl did all of the paste-up the first time. Several more helped this time.

Angela, one of only six girls on the staff, was a big help. Yesterday was also her birthday, and so I told her mine was the same day. Today she gave me a little stuffed monkey with four balloons tied to it. That gesture really touched me.

*****

Last Friday during first hour, I noticed a millipede crawling on the floor and picked it up. I made some comment appropriate to what we had been talking about and then put the critter in a film canister. I printed a "Do Not Feed" sign. Someone suggested the worm be named Leonard, so I added that to the sign.

During the next two hours, students asked about Leonard. Then some girls in fifth hour brought Leonard some weeds. I built him a cardboard house and fed him some banana chiffon cake.

Monday morning, much to our horror, we discovered that Leonard was gone. I said he had been abducted, and, from there, the insanity has snowballed.

A ransom note appeared today during first hour. Then second hour constructed a sign that said, "Day ___ of Leonard's Captivity." And while I was out of the room, a second note appeared. This one said I would receive a call at 7:55 a.m. tomorrow. It was signed "The Kidnapper."

What next?

Tuesday, October 20

I preached today. I lost my temper, and I preached. But, I must admit, I did a good job. I spoke from the heart. And I spoke sternly and decisively.

One girl in first hour is a constant complainer. She complains about assignments. She complains about tests. She complains about how boring the class is. The rest of the class has been pretty good. But I can't help but think that her whining has had a negative impact on the general attitude.

Finally, I got fed up.

I started by telling her she could leave the class if she was so unhappy with it. I told her (and the rest of the class) that I was there because I wanted to be, that I thought journalism was important, and that I was tired of whining and complaining.

I can't remember accurately the rest of what I said. But I know the words came out without being pushed. I do remember I included the fact the class is *not* a democracy and what we do or don't do is not decided by popular vote.

I think my outburst was good for the class, especially since it is the rowdiest. Most of them know I am easygoing and don't get angry often. They've made the most of that too. But now they also know I care strongly about what I do and will speak out when I have to.

*****

The kidnapper called and demanded $0.33 and a getaway car. Then a student wearing a red mask brought in another note. This one demanded $250,000.

I brought in a caterpillar named Fred to investigate the case. I told students he's a private investigator and I met him in a bar. His company is F.B.I.—Fred's Bureau of Investigation.

*****

The second newspaper looked really good, especially the layout, which was our weakest aspect last time.

We have to improve the front page now. It has been pretty dull so far.

Monday, October 26

I preached again today, this time to the newspaper staff. Stories were due, and several didn't have them. Throughout the morning, some had stopped by to offer all manner of excuses as to why they didn't have their work ready. By fifth hour, when the staff meets, I was bubbling—and not in a good way.

I told them there were no justifiable excuses for not meeting deadlines. I told them accuracy and good writing meant nothing if stories weren't ready when they were supposed to be. I told them good ideas were no better than no ideas if people didn't turn them into stories.

Several more stories were turned in before the afternoon was over.

*****

A quarter of the school year already is over. Mid-semester tests are being given this week, and grades are due next Monday.

Only four or five are failing in my classes, maybe even fewer than that.

The one who is failing the worst really bothers me. She's a freshman, and she has absolutely no concept of what is going on in class. She sits there, vegetating, almost oblivious to what is going on. It doesn't bother me that she's not enraptured by journalism. What bothers me is that she should be somewhere else, getting special help of some kind.

Her counselor told me she was placed in journalism at her own request when she transferred in. He also said to keep her there at least temporarily if she isn't causing any discipline problems. He is trying to get parental permission to have her tested for placement in special education classes.

So she sits and vegetates.

I want to say something to her. But what? What can I do for her?

She mostly likely never will be anything more than she is now. She will drop out of school. She will get pregnant. She will be on welfare.

And there's nothing I can do to help her. It just breaks my heart.

Sunday, November 1

During one of my free periods last week, I substituted for a teacher who had to leave unexpectedly. The class was Freshman English. One of my journalism students warned me the class would be "full of burnouts and blacks." And it was.

Students here seem to have segregated themselves into three groups: burnouts, soshes (from "social"), and blacks. Burnouts are those who hang around the courtyard between classes and at lunch to smoke.

Soshes wear Izod clothes, get good grades, and participate in school activities. The blacks are, well, black.

I'm afraid that I'm finding myself to be more prejudiced than I want to admit. But it's there. In the English class, the black guys really angered me. They strutted around the class like little roosters, their hands bent out at the wrists and each step an exaggerated heel-to-toe movement. They looked so ridiculous that they almost seemed comic caricatures.

One got in an immediate power struggle with me, refusing to let another student grade his paper and then jerking it away from me when I told him to let me have it. It was the first time I've really been mad since I started at Webster Groves. I don't think I could handle those kinds of students on a daily basis.

It still angers me to think about the young punks. But I also understand that they probably are that way more by circumstance and culture than by conscious choice.

Some blacks also anger me in the morning. They gather in the halls around seven thirty and start yelling obscenities at each other. I really get sick of it.

And while I'm being a bigot, I guess I should mention a girl, a senior, in one of my classes. I have about a dozen blacks in my classes, but she is the only one who speaks like she was raised in a ghetto. She constantly misuses verbs and possessives, saying such things as "they book."

The rest speak as well as their white counterparts, and I'm hopeful that at least a couple of them will want to be on the newspaper staff next year. They're good kids.

I don't want to judge and relate to my students based on skin color. People are people. Please, God, don't let me grow up to be like my mother and father.

*****

Rachel the Radical provided interesting reading in our last issue of the paper. She wanted to have an all-school assembly for some El Salvadoran rebels who are coming to this country to talk about US intervention in their country. When the principal said no to the assembly, Rachel started a petition drive.

The rebels, sponsored by the Revolutionary Communist Youth Brigade, were arrested in Oklahoma but eventually made it to St. Louis. Mr. Knight originally agreed to let them speak to special studies classes, but then withdrew that offer when he discovered their visas weren't in order.

Most of the other students don't like Rachel and don't even want to try to understand her. But she is undaunted and keeps on pushing.

It's difficult to believe she is only fifteen. I really would like to know what kind of childhood she had.

One of my students said Rachel was in Girl Scouts with her but never had anything to do with the rest of the girls and "never had any fun."

*****

We go to Kansas City Friday for a journalism convention. I will be seeing Karen, Robbie's old girlfriend, there. I'm really looking forward to that.

Tuesday, November 10

Karen and I talked for a couple of hours in a piano bar. Then we went for a carriage ride around Country Club Plaza. The air was cold, and we snuggled under a comforter. We watched puffs of steam come from the horses' nostrils and float up into the moonlight. It was like a scene out of a romantic movie.

She asked me to spend a weekend in Kansas City sometime soon and stay at her apartment. I'd like that. We get along really well together, or so it seems to me.

*****

The convention was fun. I especially enjoyed meeting advisers from other St. Louis schools.

*****

I called Connie about ten p.m. Sunday night. I don't usually call people that late but, for some reason, thought it appropriate with her. She had been a guest speaker in my classes, and I had offered to take her to lunch to show my thanks. We talked for an hour. She's going to the high school musical with me Friday night.

On Monday morning, I found a note in my mailbox at school. It said she had called on Friday and wanted me to all her Monday. ESP, maybe?

Tuesday, November 17

I wrote a long, long letter to the Mayfields more than a month ago. They never received it. I had left it in Flat River to be mailed, and my mother assured me twice that she did.

But I wonder.

I wrote another letter to the Mayfields last night, and as I was doing so, it occurred to me that Mom might have opened the letter, read it, and then threw it away. Maybe she saw a word or two—or possibly a name—through the envelope and her curiosity got the better of her.

She really resents the relationship I have with the Mayfields. I can understand her feeling that way too. She doesn't understand me. She doesn't know them. And she knows that I am closer, more intimate, with them than anyone else regarding my thoughts and feelings.

She also doesn't think I'll get back the money I loaned them four years ago. She can't understand that getting it back isn't important to me. It helped Doug,

Grace, and their four daughters through a tough time, after they took care of me when I returned to Tallahassee from Europe with a severe cause of mononucleosis. They rented a bed and put it in their living room for me. They made certain I ate well. They did my laundry. They were family.

*****

Connie was okay. I enjoyed talking with her. But I had to concentrate to keep from smirking while we made small talk in her kitchen after the musical. She goes heavy on the lipstick, too heavy. There in the kitchen, it looked like she had two upper lips.

*****

I continue to fluctuate between thinking I'm too tough and too easy as a teacher.

Third hour is consistently well behaved and work oriented. The first two hours, however, are much more volatile and noisy, and I waver on how to deal with the craziness. First hour is the least academic of the three. Second hour has a lot of smart students, but also a couple of smart mouths.

Newspaper staffers were much better about meeting their deadlines this time. But I have put one on probation. Another is doing shoddy work, and I told him that he needs to improve or take another class.

I like being a teacher.

But I hate coming home and being by myself.

I feel the desire to write, but I've been fighting it. Making journal entries helps me with that need, I think, but doesn't totally fulfill it.

Sunday, November 22

John F. Kennedy was assassinated eighteen years ago today. For me, that event seemed to signal the end of innocence. Nearly everything I remember seems to date from that time forward. But maybe it wasn't Kennedy's death as much as it was my age and the fact we had just moved from Mexico, Missouri, to Desloge, near Flat River. Maybe all three of those combined to make me more aware of the world.

I was in sophomore English class at Desloge High School when Kennedy was shot. Later, I was at my grandparents' house when Jack Ruby gunned down Lee Harvey Oswald in front of the TV cameras.

*****

Fred the caterpillar was kidnapped by assailants unknown.

Friday, the librarian, possibly the least liked and most serious person in the school, brought in a cardboard box and said it contained a replacement for

Leonard. Inside was one of the biggest roaches I've ever seen.

It was great!

I keep picturing in my head this little gray-haired lady chasing a cockroach among the shelves of books before finally waylaying it. I wonder how she caught it.

Tuesday, December 1

Racquetball season starts tomorrow. Girls asked me to be supervisor for their team, and I agreed.

*****

For some reason, I've been comparing my life now with ten years ago, when I was fresh out of the Army with a degree in journalism and ready to go to work for $135 a week as a sports writer. I don't have much to show for the past decade, except a failed marriage and a post-divorce adventure in Europe.

I want more, but I'm afraid I don't want it enough. I want it just enough to lament, but not enough to act. What good am I?

Monday, December 7

I realized something about myself today. Or at least I think I did.

Notice how I always qualify? Or nearly always?

Anyway…the realization was prompted by the announcement at school of a canned food contest. The first-hour class that brings in the most canned good for charity wins. One teacher, Mr. Brucker, wins every year—or so the students say. They told me that last year his students brought in thousands of cans.

The winning class receives McDonald's coupons, but at just one dollar per student, that can't be the motivating factor for his students.

It's good for charity that his class does so much. But at the same time, other classes must be demoralized. Supposedly, his students bring in more cans than all the other classes combined.

What would it be like to challenge his class, I wondered. But then I realized I didn't want to do that. First, my class wouldn't have a chance. More importantly, however, is the tradition involved. And why rock the boat when so much good is being done for charity?

But still …

These thoughts about competition somehow made me realize I like sport for the sport, not for winning or any masochistic fulfillment that losing provides.

I know I've always told myself this. But for some reason, I believe it more now than I ever have before. I always thought of myself as a passive person and, consequently, a defensive player, especially in sports such as tennis, ping pong, and racquetball.

Now I realize that I play defensively because I want to prolong the game. I truly enjoy the competition more than the final result. I always hope for extra innings.

This is no big deal, I know. But I feel wiser about myself, nonetheless.

And speaking of racquetball, the girls' team got clobbered in its first match.

Wednesday, December 9

But they won today.

It wasn't because of my managerial expertise or because I gave them a stirring pep talk either. I'm just there because a faculty supervisor is required.

*****

It occurs to me that I convey impressions or opinions to my students that I don't intend. This happens because of the inadequacy of words as a means of communication. It also happens because students listen but don't always hear. Their minds wander.

Realization about the former, however, touches me much deeper than does the latter.

I started thinking about this after I discussed public reaction to John Lennon's death a year ago. I mentioned what a profound influence that I thought he had on music and life since the 1960s. And I talked about how upset much of Middle America was that his death received so much attention. If anything, I thought I sounded favorable to Lennon, but that's not the way some of them heard it.

And a few weeks ago, I discovered that some of my students thought I favored more controls on the press because I mentioned the bad with the good of the media. Nothing could be further from the truth.

So I wonder…Is this the way of the world? Thoughts, opinions, and prejudices are inferred as much by miscommunication as communication?

Saturday, December 12

Mr. Knight told me Thursday I probably will have my job next year. Also, I might be adviser for the yearbook. I think I would like to stay at Webster Groves for three years and then move on.

Teaching still seems wonderfully fulfilling, yet occasionally frustrating. First hour is my biggest source of frustration. Three or four kids talk too much, and that class in general is lower academically than the other two. Yet I like the kids in that class as much as in the other two. They simply aren't interested in journalism.

Individual classes, I'm beginning to see, have unique personalities, just like people.

*****

I called Connie Thursday night. I told her that I was poor. She said that it didn't matter. We're getting together next weekend.

Thursday, December 17

I know what traditionalists must have felt like when the car started replacing the horse as the major means of transportation.

Maybe I am thinking about it now because video games are being pushed so heavily right now as Christmas gifts. It's impossible to watch TV without seeing commercials for them. They are prominently displayed in stores. And along with sex and alcohol, they're a favorite topic of conversation for teenagers.

Home computers have joined the ranks too, along with pocket calculators, and VCRs. Banks are computerized. Newspapers and schools are computerized. And 1984 still is more than two years away.

I guess Man always is uncomfortable with the new, especially when it varies considerably from what he knew as a child.

*****

I realized that I've probably been too lenient with first hour when I heard one of the few students who seems interested in learning say the class has a "lack of respect."

Yesterday I put the attentive students (about ten) in front and the noisiest (about five) in the back. I told them I was segregating them by how disruptive they were in class. I told the ones in back that they could move to the front if they felt like working and those in front that they could move to the back if they didn't. No one moved, and the class was quiet for the rest of the hour.

Today the class was quieter than usual too, but still there was noise. The kids in front, however, told those in back to shut up. No one had done anything like that before. Or at least it hadn't been done so noticeably.

Also, one of the girls in back moved to the front.

Whatever else that class might be, it's certainly a learning experience for me.

*****

I put up a Christmas tree. The students brought in lights, tinsel, and ornaments from home.

Friday, December 25, Christmas Day

Our twelve-page paper looked good, and it sold better than any of the earlier issues. We got a lot of good comments about the articles. But Mr. Knight, the principal, didn't like the paper. Too negative, he said.

I think he was turned off by the editorial, which was about the high cost of being a senior, and a satire about relatives at Christmas.

The staff had a Christmas party Wednesday afternoon. I'm afraid I let the kids be too rambunctious. But at least when the principal stopped by, the music was off and the guys had stopped playing football with an orange.

*****

I felt tired and inferior for several days before Christmas break. Kids were restless, and that contributed to a lot of my negative feelings, I'm sure. I hope the time before every vacation isn't like that.

*****

Chris, who probably is a genius, nearly caused in riot in third hour Tuesday when he drew a Japanese flag and wrote "Celebrate Pearl Harbor Day" on the blackboard. One of the boys immediately confronted him, and two of the girls erased his work with their fingers.

After class, I told Chris to stay, and we talked. He told me that the other students weren't acting rationally because Japan suffered as much as we did because of Hiroshima and Nagasaki. Although I was tempted, I didn't counter with the fact that Japan initiated war against our country with its attack on Pearl Harbor.

Instead, I ignored his own irrationality and told him the world does not respond to most of life in a rational matter. I told him people are much more emotional than rational and he must get used to it. I also told him that the others know he is smarter than they and interpret much of what he does as arrogance.

He said he likes to annoy people and added that one student threatened him with a knife last year. He insisted, however, that no danger is involved in what he is doing.

I told him it is easy to lose perspective if you do something long enough, to forget you are vulnerable. I equated what he was doing with those who drive recklessly because they don't realize how dangerous cars can be.

I think he got something out of our talk. I hope so, anyway.

The next day, he indirectly apologized and said that he had been conducting an experiment.

*****

I saw Connie Saturday night and then had dinner at her house Tuesday. I like her. But she is too formal, too made-up for my liking. She always looks as if she is ready to go before a camera. We share interest in the media but little else, I think.

On Tuesday we talked about television. I told her that I really didn't care if I had a TV, but my mother always made certain I did.

*****

Until today, I was using an old set that belongs to Craig. Mom and Dad gave me a new one for Christmas.

I never said, or even hinted, that I wanted one. I said I wanted a Hudson Bay blanket. But I knew my mother didn't like that idea. She said it cost too much, although it actually was less than a television, and told me it would be "too hard to clean."

So she got me what I really needed—a television set.

*****

Two friends back home are having marital problems. Both married young, and now they are restless and bored. Although they don't say so directly, I receive the distinct impression that they envy me because I'm single. One of them said that he wanted to "sneak out and go to a couple of bars" with me. I've told them that I know from personal experience that divorce is a rough road and they should be careful about moving in that direction, especially since both have children.

Maybe Man's recent realization of the many options life holds will eventually lead to a fulfillment never before realized. But right now that realization seems to provide more restlessness and unhappiness than anything else. That doesn't mean I think ignorance is bliss. Rather, transition is hell.

1982

Saturday, January 9

About two a.m. one night last week, I awoke to the sounds of a man crying. He lives in the other half of this duplex. He cried long and loud. Finally, his wife said, "Oh, stop crying."

"All I can do is cry," he sobbed.

"That's all you can do. That's all anyone can do," she replied.

I think she must have told him that she wants a separation or divorce. Why else would she have been so unsympathetic?

I felt very uncomfortable listening. It reminded me that the same thing had happened in an apartment in Tallahassee in March of 1976. I cried long and loud when Lois said that, yes, she was certain she wanted a divorce. Only Lois was more sympathetic than the woman next door.

I wonder if anyone heard us the way I heard the people next door.

*****

The Webster Groves school district is having a tax levy election on February 2. We're coming out with a special edition of the paper that will tell all about the levy and what might happen if it fails. What might happen is that several teachers probably will lose their jobs.

*****

I heard third-hand that Vicki, the music teacher, would like to go out with me.

Sharon called Wednesday from Canada, and it sure was good to talk to her. We've stayed in touch since we met in Paris back in late 1976. I told her that I would like to visit her this summer. She suggested that we might drive a thousand miles farther north to Yellowknife in the Northwest Territories. I really would like to have another adventure with her.

*****

Connie and I went out last Saturday night. After going to a movie, we went back to her house, sat on the sofa, and talked for three hours. Finally, I got up enough nerve to kiss her.

We kissed and held each other for more than an hour. That was the most sexually aroused I've been in quite a while. I felt alive again.

I told Connie that I felt like a teenager. I was afraid that telling her anything more might frighten her.

*****

No date this weekend. I had thought I was going to Kansas City to see Karen. But when I called her on Thursday, she said she had made other plans since she hadn't heard from me. That was the second time that we've made plans for me to visit and then she has been busy at the last minute.

She asked about next weekend. I said I had plans, even though I don't. I suspect that all I'll have to remember about Karen is that romantic carriage ride.

Thursday, January 14

During second hour, a girl asked if she could speak to me privately. As soon as we were alone, she started crying. She said she had a problem at home and wanted to know if she could hand in an assignment late.

I immediately said, "yes," and added that she didn't have to talk about it if she didn't want to.

Heartfelt

She wanted to talk. Her mother is an alcoholic, she said, and she lives alone with her since she is an only child and her parents are divorced. Her mother is a first-grade teacher but hasn't been able to stay sober long enough to keep a job. She said "things" have been really bad at home.

I wanted to cry with her, but we had to get back to class.

I felt so sad and yet so grateful that she confided in me and I might have lessened a little of her suffering. That is what being a teacher is all about.

*****

Then came fifth hour. A boy wanted to know if his grade is suffering. He said he knows it is in other classes, and the reason is a problem at home. His parents are splitting.

He said that worries about that makes it difficult for him to concentrate. But at the same time, he tried to make light of his concerns, laughing and saying, "I'll be all right."

I told him I noticed that, at times, he seemed preoccupied, but still he is doing more than his share and his grade won't suffer.

A few weeks ago, I wrote him a note, telling him that I was disappointed because he hadn't followed through on an assignment. I've found that I do that with kids who have potential. I like them more. I expect more out of them. I let them know when I'm not happy. Thus far, they've responded positively.

Tuesday, January 26

It's funny. First hour gives me the most headaches. But I really like some of the kids in that class, including some of the noisiest.

One of them is Michelle. She's very dramatic and flamboyant. I really yelled at her a couple of weeks ago. She's a little quieter now, but still loud and distracting.

I realize that noise and disruption simply is a part of who she is, but I have an obligation to teach, and she sometimes makes it difficult. If only she were obnoxious, I wouldn't have any difficulty shutting her up. But, dammit, she's so entertaining.

Tuesday, February 2

Last Saturday evening, I left home to pick up Connie for dinner at the home of one of her friends, who had an indoor pool. I got back at two thirty this afternoon. Yes, that's right. We had a three-day date.

As I drove, I heard a forecast that called for rain changing to freezing drizzle and "maybe a few snow flurries." No mention was made of accumulation.

But heavy snow was pelting down by the time I reached Connie's house, and driving conditions deteriorated so quickly that we decided not to try to get to her friend's place. By Sunday evening, when the storm finally ended, we had two feet of snow. Parked along the side of the street, my little MG Midget was completely buried by the drifts from this "worst storm in seventy years."

Of course I had no boots or heavy clothing either. I was dressed for the weather that we were forecast to have, not what we received.

One of Connie's neighbors gave me a pair of her husband's old boots, complete with a hole in one toe. But they were far better than the Sperry Top-Siders I wore in anticipation of a casual evening around her friend's pool.

On Monday, we walked to downtown Webster. All the stores were closed except a grocery store and Velvet Freeze. After food shopping, we bought ice cream cones and trudged back to her place.

Schools were closed all over St. Louis, and even the mail couldn't be delivered. The National Guard was called to help clear the roads.

Even now, many streets and highways are treacherous. It took me more than an hour to drive fifteen miles this afternoon, and I hate to think what it will be like at rush hour tomorrow morning when it is supposed to be snowing again.

The snow was beautiful, coming down in enormous, wet flakes and sticking to everything. Saturday night, it was accompanied by thunder and lightning.

Seeing lightning in a snowstorm is totally unlike seeing it during a summer thunderstorm. Reflected against the white, it seems an enormous camera flash. Also, there's no sense of danger because it doesn't happen often enough in winter for fear to be developed.

A big pine tree in my neighbor's yard split and broke under the weight of the snow. Or maybe lightning hit it.

Before driving home, I shoveled out my car and Connie's driveway. Then I had to shovel out my drive to get my car into the garage. I'm not too tired, but I'll bet I sleep well.

I didn't sleep well at Connie's. I rarely do in unaccustomed surroundings. I really didn't enjoy being there either, although I like Connie.

That much time together really highlights how little we have in common. She spends hours and hours each day fixing her hair and makeup. She wears high-heeled boots to walk in the snow and leaves her dress coat fashionably open at the neck, no matter how wet and cold she gets.

Also, I was very uncomfortable around her housemate, Beth, who owns the house where they live. Beth seems to be a cold, unhappy person. Her life is her job, which is teaching.

And, no, with Beth around, Connie and I didn't pick up where we left off that night on her sofa. I made no move, and neither did she.

Sunday, February 7

Tax levy failed by about one hundred and fifty votes. Two-thirds majority was required. About two dozen teachers, including me, could lose their jobs.

*****

I've felt a sadness since leaving Connie's, an emptiness. I knew that we didn't share a lot of interests, even before I was stranded at her house. But until the snowstorm, at least there was hope. Saying that now and seeing it in myself, I realize how much I want to be with a woman.

Now hope has been shattered by the reality that I didn't enjoy my time with her. There's no hope for us.

Beth depressed me too. She just doesn't relate to people very well. I overheard her giving Connie directions on how they were going to clean the house while they were snowed in. The thought of those two alone in that big house saddens me.

Of course the thought of me alone in this duplex would sadden a lot of people, including me.

I don't want Valentine's Day to come because it will require some action on my part toward Connie. Either I intentionally will ignore the day or I will not. I don't want to do either. I just want it to go away.

Since the arrival of all this unhappiness, I've started thinking about moving back to Flat River.

Maybe that's standard procedure for me: pack up and go home when the world isn't the way I want it to be. Maybe recognizing this tendency will help me overcome it.

Or maybe I don't want to.

*****

I went to Flat River on Friday because I couldn't stand being cooped up here any longer. We didn't have school all week, which was unprecedented for Webster Grove schools, since so few students take buses.

On Wednesday and Thursday, I sent out articles and query letters and did some cooking and cleaning.

We were supposed to have more snow Friday morning, but it missed us, so I headed south.

St. Louis still is digging out, and city schools will be closed again tomorrow. Cleanup cost for the thirty-county portion of the state hit by the storm is estimated at $4 million.

I'm sure we will have school tomorrow, and I'm eager to get back.

Wednesday, February 17

I still haven't called Connie. Don't know if I will.

*****

Nearly half of my fifty-six journalism students asked to be on the newspaper staff next year. I had planned to take fewer than eighteen, the number on this year's staff. But I accepted twenty-one. I just couldn't say no to some of them. Everyone I took is an A or B student and, I believe, will do all right on the staff.

Mr. Knight told me that the job is mine for next year, no matter what happens with another tax levy proposal for April 6.

He sat in on my first-hour class this morning. Normally it is the noisiest. Today it was the quietest—even after he left.

*****

My sister Rhonda's collie, Mandy, had five puppies on Valentine's Day. No one knew she was pregnant. The father has not come forth. He is believed to be a German shepherd.

Thursday, February 18

It appears Chris didn't learn anything from me about the dangers of arrogance, and he paid the price.

He was unhappy with an illustration that accompanied his article in the *Echo*. In response, he wrote a letter to the editor, criticizing *all* the illustrations.

Since he is a sophomore and not on the staff, members didn't want to run his story in the first place. In doing so, they figured they were doing him a favor.

When they saw Chris's letter, several of them went berserk. Today, three of them, wearing paper bag masks, marched into my third-hour class and planted shaving-cream pies in his face.

Then it was Chris's turn to go berserk. He chased and caught one of the masked marauders. Fortunately, I got there about the same time, as did the football coach. The hall around us was packed with people, since the attack occurred only seconds before class ended.

The other two pie-men escaped.

The football coach called the janitor to clean up. I said that I'd take care of reporting the incident.

Chris had shaving cream all over his face, hair, and shoulders. Several who had been sitting near him were splattered too, as was much of the classroom. The whole place reeked of mint.

Chris said he wasn't mad after he got cleaned up. Actually, he fared better than Carl, the one he caught. Somehow, the front of Carl's jeans got a large tear during the scuffle.

When I called to report the incident, the secretary asked who got hit. After I told her, she laughed and said, "He probably deserved it."

I suspect many of those at Webster feel the same way. Chris is just too arrogant for his own good.

I'm not sure how I feel about what happened. I knew it was going to, and I did nothing to discourage it. I was afraid Chris would do exactly what he did. Who wouldn't?

But I also was reluctant to say, "no." I might even have encouraged the incident as a lesson for Chris, showing him that arrogant actions can have serious consequences.

Also, it was fun. The next day, I instructed students to write about the attack to test their powers of observation.

I'm sure Chris now is planning his revenge.

I have told both sides that I will allow no more such actions in my classes. I guess that means I wish I hadn't allowed it in the first place. Or maybe I've learned my lesson.

*****

I still haven't called Connie. Nor have I asked out Vicki, the music teacher.

*****

Charlie B. called Monday and asked me to ride to the airport with him to pick up something. I went, although I knew why he was going, and I felt a little funny about it. What else would a mortician pick up at the airport?

It cost more to ship the body air freight from San Francisco than it would have to buy it a coach-fare ticket. That doesn't seem right.

The three of us then headed for my duplex. Charlie and I did most of the talking. With just the two of them, I suspect the remainder of the drive back to his funeral home in Desloge was pretty quiet.

Monday, February 22

A senior at another school was murdered last week while working at a gas station. As usual, some students tried to crack jokes about tragedy as we discussed the killing. I told them the discussion this time had no place for humor.

Are they really so callous and uncaring? Will they grow up to be callous and uncaring adults? Or is it just a phase, something a few of them do in the same way they make fun of anyone who shows a sincere interest or concern about someone or something? I have to believe it's a phase.

*****

Scott's stepfather met with me the other day, at his request. Scott is one of the noisiest in my first-hour class.

I now feel much more sympathetic toward Scott. His stepfather talks a lot but does little listening. I'm sure he's the same way with Scott, who probably is attention starved. His father seems a pusher and a punisher, not a parent and a praiser.

Wednesday, March 10

I put the top down on my car today. The sun and the wind seemed to fill me with new life. I can't wait to start gardening and softball.

Connie called the other night. I think she called to tell me about her new job at a cable company. I don't think we'll go out again.

Sunday, March 21

I received a letter Friday, saying that I probably won't be offered a contract for next year. Eighteen other probationary teachers at the high school did too. If the April 6 levy proposal fails, twelve will lose their jobs. If it passes, five will.

Mr. Knight assured me that he is trying his best to keep me. He gave me my final evaluation last week and told me that I have done an outstanding job.

He seems confident that I will be rehired. I don't feel so confident. For one thing, the woman I replaced is coming back. The principal said he wants to keep me in journalism and put her elsewhere. But it looks to me as if I should be one of the first to go since she also is qualified to each journalism.

Wednesday, March 24

My article about catching catfish by hand—"hogging"—is "too repugnant a topic" for *Sports Illustrated*, according to a rejection I received. The funny thing is that comment came from an editor who replaced an editor who asked to see the piece. Oh, well . . . So much of success and happiness in life is about connecting with the right person at the right time.

I've sent it to *Southern Outdoors Magazine*, which I'm hopeful will be more receptive.

*****

I became an uncle for the second time at eleven forty-five a.m. today. Judy gave birth to Monica Marie after about ten hours of labor. Craig called about forty thirty to tell me. He still hadn't come back down to earth.

Then Mom called to tell me that the baby "looks just like Craig's baby pictures."

Craig watched the birth. In the past, he nearly fainted at the sight of blood. I guess he's moved past that. I'm happy for them, though it's hard to believe my baby brother has a baby.

Sunday, March 28

Four English teachers at the high school will lose their jobs. I will be one of them. Even if the tax levy passes, I still could not be rehired. Mr. Knight gave me that assessment Thursday.

I am expecting the worst.

Sunday, April 4

I'm attracted to some of the senior girls in my classes. No doubt spring has something to do with that. Also, I've now known them for seven months. Familiarity is an important element for me to be drawn to a woman.

But I would never make any advances toward my students. If I had become a teacher at age twenty-one or twenty-two, I don't think I would have either. But who knows how forward some of those girls might have been if I were just three or four years older. And how I would have responded.

Bottom line is that I'm an authority figure and role model, not a friend or peer.

Wednesday, April 7

The tax levy failed.

I will now have to start looking for another job. I want to find one quickly because I won't feel much like job hunting as the end of school nears. I'm afraid I'll be too depressed if I wait. I'm really going to miss some of the kids.

Again I'm a nomad, as I have been since my divorce in 1976. A new job. A new place to live. The stress of starting over. I'm really getting tired. I was looking forward to being at Webster Groves for more than one year. It seemed so right.

Monday, April 12

I'm depressed. Just spent more than four hundred dollars on car repairs. I'm back to no money, along with no job. I feel really helpless, vulnerable, lost.

On the bright side, *Southern Outdoors* says it will buy my article about catching catfish by hand. That would be my first freelance sale to a major magazine!

I'll believe it when I receive the payment.

I almost forgot the worst blow of all during this bleak time. I broke my Miss Piggy glass.

Tuesday, April 13

I received official notification today that I have been "terminated" as of June 10. I'm certainly not alone. Teachers all over St. Louis County got the same news because of public education's financial problems.

But I feel alone. I don't mind losing the job so much. I can find another. I hate to leave my students, though. We've spent a year getting to know each other. I like them. I think they like me. Now I have to go through another year of getting acquainted. And I have to say goodbye to some really good kids. It hurts.

The Parkway District has a journalism opening, so I guess I'll apply there. I hear that it's a good system.

*****

Some of the kids have talked about starting a petition to keep me at Webster. Their loyalty is one of the great things about teaching, although I realize they probably would feel that way about most any teacher. They know me. They're comfortable with me. And now someone they don't know is taking over. What's known is almost always preferred to what's unknown.

*****

Hearing of my tragedy, the yearbook staff gave me a new Miss Piggy glass. I don't teach that class, but it meets in my room and I talk with the students quite a bit. They like me too, I guess.

Wednesday, April 21

Robbie called from New York City. He said he was calling to tell me he wouldn't be in St. Louis in May after all. But I think he also wanted to speak with someone who understands his frustrations.

We talked for nearly an hour and a half. Or rather, Robbie talked. I listened. He told me he feels "really beaten down" because he's been in NYC for nearly three years and has little to show for it. He's making money doing PR jobs and special media projects, but he wants a career in TV and movies.

He said NYC is a city of illusions, or, rather, business is all illusion. Nothing is what it seems. "The 'stars,'" he said, "are just like you and me, only they chose different occupations. And they're neurotic. Real neurotic."

In an earlier conversation, Robbie had encouraged me to join him in New York. "You're just a talented as the people here," he said then. "The only difference is that you're there and they're here."

This time, he talked about writing for *The David Letterman Show*. He said Letterman "loved" his writing, but they didn't "hit it off."

I told him I understand his frustrations and that I have a dream too. I want to be a writer. I told him that we must not know ourselves as well as we often think we do, that there is something that keeps pushing us and that keeps us reaching, clawing, and climbing. Maybe that thing, whatever it is, knows us better than we do, knows that we would shrivel and dry up if we were to stop dreaming and driving.

He identified with that. He said he looks for signs to tell him to stop, that he's no good, that he's wasting his time. But the signs aren't there. Or maybe that "thing" won't let him see them. He can't quit. He has no reason to. He knows he's good. He has to keep reaching.

*****

Lately, I've felt this urge to read my journal. Why? But I'm afraid. Why?

Sunday, April 25

Sunday evening is the most depressing time of the week for me. I feel empty, lethargic. Nothing sounds appealing. But at least I recognize that this is tied to a time and not to a specific issue that is troubling me. It's something I can live through until it goes away on Monday morning.

*****

I recently attended what was called a party, presented by Sponsors of School Publications. But there was nothing festive about it.

As I sat there and listened to three or four simultaneous conversations, all of them negative, I wondered what I was doing trying to be a teacher. And it's not just about low pay and stressful working conditions either.

I haven't been very impressed by the teachers I've met this year. The Webster drama teacher, Ron Kenney, is the only one I respect. Most of the rest seem to be gray, rather nondescript creatures. And I guess I'm afraid of being the same way by association—if I'm not that way already.

*****

Last Thursday as I was leaving the classroom, I reminded yearbook sponsor Ron Carr that he had left a large, black plastic top for a spray can on the podium. He said with mock solemnity, "Don't move that whatever you do."

I printed a "Danger! Don't lift!" sign and taped it to the top.

All the next day, that top provided an excellent study in human behavior. I could have predicted who would be the first students to look, and they proved me correct.

Others gave the sign a little more consideration. They sat or stood by the podium and quizzed me as they fingered the top. Not one who touched it, I noticed, could leave without lifting it. But not every student was compelled to touch it. One made an elaborate production out of telling me how he always obeyed signs like that.

During second hour, my favorite class, the students came up one at a time to look. Not one of those who looked would tell the others that nothing was under the plastic top.

Monday, April 26

The *Echo* earned All-Missouri honors from the Missouri Interscholastic Press Association. Our paper and Kirkwood's were the only St. Louis area schools to win this highest recognition. We also received a first place for our in-depth tax levy special edition, as well as a first in news, third in features, and honorable mention in editorial writing.

I'll bet I'm the only sponsor of an All-Missouri paper looking for a job.

One of my students said, "Well, I guess you'll just have to make some other paper the best in the state." That really made me feel good.

Not once had I said I have such an ambition. But I guess my insistence on quality and getting it right made students realize that I expected a lot out of them.

*****

I finally had to get tough with Paul in first hour. He's intelligent and creative. But he's also childish and disruptive. I told him exactly that when I removed him from class for two days.

Yesterday he said something really off-color, which had nothing to do with class. I deliberated overnight about what to do so I wouldn't act out of anger.

I told Paul that I wasn't mad at him but that I was very tired of his behavior. I also warned him that I would remove him from class permanently if he said something similar again.

I don't remember precisely what he said, but it had something to do with me "stuffing" my swim trunks when I go to the beach in the summer.

Also in first hour, I've noticed a recent disturbing trend. Some of the students who used to be quiet now are disruptive.

Maybe it's just the fact that it's spring and school will be out soon. But maybe they're doing it because noisy kids get more attention, even if it is negative, and, for some, even that kind of attention is better than none at all.

Sunday, May 9

Parkway North High School all but offered me the job. I go back Tuesday afternoon.

Three people interviewed me. I think I did well with the principal and assistant principal. But I was a little uncomfortable with the English Department chairman. My mind has been focused on journalism only for a year, and I had given no thought to teaching English until he was drilling me, asking me about such things as "modernists."

I did make one lucky response, though, when he asked who I would include in a study of literature. I said Salinger and *The Catcher in the Rye*. He then told me that book is one of the required novels for Sophomore English, which I would be teaching.

I guess I should be excited about the job. Several people have told me that Parkway is *the* place to work. But I'm still too sad about leaving Webster to get too excited.

*****

I met the mother of one of next year's editors at a soccer game Friday. She said that my leaving will "leave a deep gulf in Angela's life."

*****

My letter to the local weekly newspaper was just published. I said, "I am one of several teachers who will not be returning to Webster Groves because the tax levy failed. During my too short year there, I found the students to be more than a pleasure to teach. They are a joy to know. I will miss them."

Tuesday, May 11

Parkway North offered me the job of newspaper and yearbook adviser, as well as English and journalism teacher. It sounds like a lot more work than I am doing now.

On the positive side, the facilities are light-years ahead of those at Webster. Also, the pay is more.

When I walked into the North office this afternoon, Paul Delanty, the assistant principal, immediate asked if I also had an appointment with Parkway Central, another high school in the district. It seems someone there also saw my application and mentioned it to him.

Sunday, May 23

Keith, the best writer on the *Echo* staff, wrote all sorts of "clever" things in my yearbook.

I didn't mind him having fun at my expense. In fact, I would have been disappointed if he didn't. But he went too far when he mentioned Angela, one of next year's editors.

For months now, he and several others have been implying that I favor Angela because she "favors" me. Of course, they do it behind her back.

In my yearbook, Keith put a halo over her head and he made the boy in the photo next to hers a doctor saying, "Hey, Angela, the rabbit died."

"Someone" then put the page number of the work of art on the first page of the yearbook so everyone opening the book immediately sees it and turns there.

Of course, all of this was done when I wasn't looking.

I told Keith that he might be able to write better than many adults, but he certainly doesn't have the maturity of one. I told him that what he did was childish and cruel. I emphasized that I didn't mind him having fun with me, but he had no business ridiculing Angela and then advertising it on the front page.

He said he didn't put the page number on the front page. I told him I expected that and that I also expected he wouldn't tell me who did. That being the case, I added, he could relay the message about my disappointment and disgust with the cruel prank.

Later, Keith told me he felt "really bad." I said, "Good." I also told him I didn't dislike him, only what he did.

I almost believe he was sincere about feeling bad.

Thursday, June 3

Yesterday I wrote Mr. Knight a note, asking him if my fifth-hour newspaper class could play softball today since we are finished for the year. His reply: "This is one of those things that it is better not to ask about."

So what does that mean? Does it mean we shouldn't do it? Or does it mean do it but don't talk about it?

That note definitely goes in the book!

Finals start Monday. Tomorrow is the last regular day of class. I think I'm going to be really depressed about this time next week.

I stopped by Parkway North this afternoon. The thought of starting over, and with yearbook this time, really is almost overwhelming.

*****

I made plane reservations for Florida and Canada. Features editor at the *Post-Dispatch* expressed interest in a couple of my article ideas related to the Canada trip, including the Calgary Stampede.

I've sold several articles to the newspaper this past year, but my goal is to get published in magazines. My hope is that sale to *Southern Outdoors* is just the start, instead of a one-time thing.

Sunday, June 6

Now I better understand that cryptic reply from Mr. Knight regarding my request for the *Echo* staff to play softball. On Friday, the final day for regular classes, teachers and administrators patrolled the halls as never before. They manned the cafeteria in force to prevent food fights.

Kids set off fireworks in the courtyard and halls, evading capture.

One of the seniors said "Have a helluva day!" as he finished reading the morning announcements a week ago Friday. After being suspended for three days, he apologized over the public address system and was allowed to come back to school.

So far, there has been no senior prank, which evidently is a tradition. One teacher told me that this is the quietest end of school he has seen in years.

*****

I told second hour that it was my favorite journalism class of the year. I said that it was my favorite not only because students showed consideration for me but for each other. A few thought I said that to all my classes. I assured them I did not.

What I said is true. Some students in first hour were rude and immature. In third hour, Chris created dissension. Only in second hour was everyone mature enough to get along.

I will miss them all.

I guess one gets used to saying goodbye to students as the years pass, and the pain lessens. But this year was my first, and it hurts.

Still, I don't want to get used to it. I don't want to feel less than I do now. The pain I feel is exquisite pain.

Ron, an immensely talented young man, told me he learned more working on the paper than he did in any other class. We were both a little choked up as we said goodbye on Friday, the seniors' last day.

A few others said similar things. But his words touched me the deepest.

I praised him often throughout the year. But I also was hard on him at times. Also, I criticized some of his cartoons and often had them changed because I felt they hurt or antagonized needlessly.

I always tried to explain my reasoning to him, and, I guess, if he wasn't convinced, he at least understood my point of view. I also frequently defended his cartoons when teachers and administrators said, "I don't understand it. Why do you run it?"

*****

I felt pain of another kind in Flat River this weekend when I told Mom I was going to visit the Mayfields and Dave and Shirley in Florida, starting June 14.

She pulled out a piece of paper and said, "I found that letter the other day that Grace sent, saying they were going to pay you as soon as they sold their house, if you want to take it with you."

Then she smiled a hateful smile, trying to make it look as if she were joking.

While I was there, Grace called. Mother answered. After I took the phone, Grace asked what was wrong. She said Mom was very cold. She then guessed what was wrong.

What's wrong is that Mom is jealous of the affection I feel for the Mayfields, and the money they owe me is a way for her to focus her resentment toward them.

It really came as a shock to me a few years ago when I first saw the hostility she had for them, after they didn't immediately pay me back. She knows how much they have done for me.

Now I am no longer shocked by her cruel jealousy. But still it hurts, as did the fact that she obviously went through my personal possessions to find that letter.

Friday, June 11

I was near tears most of Thursday morning.

Checkout at school was eleven a.m., and I went around saying my goodbyes until then. One of the assistant principals said that Vicki, the music teacher, and I were the school's "superstars" and "We expect to hear a lot more about you."

The kids weren't there Thursday, which made leaving easier. I told Ron, the drama teacher, how hard it was to say goodbye to them. He said it was that way for him for ten years. Then he started looking forward to seeing them go.

I think the year was a good one for me professionally. Even though I still want to write, I feel much better about myself as a teacher than I ever did as a newspaper reporter/features writer. At school, I felt I was making the world a better place, or at least trying my best to do that.

Seeing my name in print regularly was good for my ego, but it never gave me the inner warmth I got from teaching.

Next year, however, I have to start all over at a new school with a lot of added responsibilities. I'll be okay, I guess.

*****

But now it's summer. Monday I leave for Florida. Then I go to Canada on July 6. Sharon called earlier this week, and it really was exciting to talk to her. This will be the first traveling I've done in two years.

Monday, June 28, Flat River

Last night I returned from two weeks in Florida. I spent three days with Dave and Shirley in Tampa and the rest of the time with the Mayfields in Miami. I last saw D&S (in Tampa) in the summer of 1980. I hadn't been to Miami since November 1979.

We laughed a lot and ate a lot in Tampa—the typical way we spend time when I visit. We also went to a seabird sanctuary on a terribly rainy day, and I took photos for a possible feature for the *Post*.

On my last day in Tampa, I called Grace and told her that I thought I would delay going to Miami for one day. She exploded. She told me about all the plans she had made and how inconsiderate I was. I immediately said I would *not* change my arrival date after all, but she didn't seem to care. She just kept berating.

I said, "Goodbye, Grace" and hung up.

We went out to dinner. What I really wanted was withdraw into a corner somewhere and not do anything. But I fought the urge and talked to D&S about it.

When we returned from dinner, I called Grace again. She was much calmer this time. She said she even called my parents to get the number where I was staying. All was forgiven. I told her that the first call hadn't scared me away, that I had decided I was going to Miami no matter how mad she was at me.

I learned a lot about myself from the phone episode. I learned that I no longer am afraid of losing Grace's love when she gets mad at me. When I lived in Miami with her family, I knew that intellectually, of course, but emotionally she terrified me, and I withdrew. That dynamic helped me decide to move back to Missouri in September 1979, after I helped them move to Miami in July and stayed awhile to explore, fish, and work construction.

This time I fought the urge to withdraw, and by the time Dave, Shirley, and I finished dinner, I was eager to call Grace back and take the offensive.

*****

The love shown me in Miami was almost overwhelming. I told Grace how wonderful it was and how much it meant to me. I even said "I love you" to Mom when I called home. That's something I can't say to my family when I'm in Flat River, Missouri.

My first night in Miami, the huskies escaped from the yard. Doug and I found Shilka about an hour after they got out. But we jogged for three hours up and down the canals and never found C.K. We finally gave up about three thirty a.m.

At about one p.m. the next day, I was sitting in the living room with the twins, Rachel and Rebecca. Rachel asked if I thought C.K. would be able to return on his own, and I said, "no."

Then, suddenly, I felt the urge to go to the front door. I did so slowly, almost nonchalantly. I opened it, and there stood C.K., shivering in the rain. I experienced no surprise. I simply called to him quietly and calmly so he would come in. It was almost as if my subconscious knew he was there. ESP? Intuition? I don't what it was. But it was something.

I met Linda's husband, Felix. He's the grandson of Batista, a former Cuban dictator. I don't like him. He shows almost no love for Linda at all. He's nervous and superficial. He had lived at home and never worked before marrying Linda. That wouldn't seem too bad if he were twenty-one. But he's thirty.

He was under psychiatric care for a while and took anti-depressant medication. His brother is a drug dealer. One of his friends has been in twenty-seven different mental institutions, according to Linda. A wonderful bunch of people.

Linda is expecting a baby in November. She's working at TG&Y, a department store in Orlando. Felix is a waiter at Disney World. Linda has more talent for more things than anyone I've ever met, including art, math, and tennis. Yet now there's a good chance she will never make use of any of her potential.

Grace and Doug don't think the marriage will last. They hope it doesn't. But Grace also is afraid Linda will move back home, return to school, and she (Grace) will be given the responsibility of raising another child. She says she doesn't want to raise another because four daughters was enough.

Grace still has all sorts of health problems. Allergies, heart, hearing, etc. Also, she put on weight. I'm worried about her.

At long last, I met Sheila. In fact, I think we saw each other every day I was there. She's twenty-nine, intelligent, considerate almost to a fault, but not afraid to speak up or disagree. I like her. She likes me. In August, she might come visit me in Missouri.

Sheila even went on an all-night fishing trip with me Friday. Originally, only Rebecca and George, Rebecca's boyfriend, were going. Then four Turkish guys from the office where Grace works at the University of Miami asked to go with us. Then Grace talked Sheila into going. Only George and I had any fishing experience.

But we all had fun. The seas were calm, the air was warm, and the fish were biting. We caught grouper and snapper. Rebecca fished all night. Sheila tried to stay with it but fought a mild case of seasickness most of the time. I don't think she would go on such a trip again. But, still, she tried.

George likes to fish as much as I do. He's also a clown. I really like him. He and Rebecca seem to belong together.

George works with bees. I went with him one day to watch. I put on the cotton suit, head net, rubber gloves, etc. But still it was scary to hear bees buzzing all around. George wears a suit and net but no gloves. He's developed an immunity to bee stings, he said. He was stung three times the day I went with him.

Midnight, Monday, July 12, Yellowknife, Northwest Territories

I arrived in Canada last Tuesday, landing in Edmonton, Alberta. Sharon Doktycz, a girl I met in Europe in 1976, lives there. On Thursday, we drove to Barrhead, a city about ninety miles north, to visit her sister's family. On Friday, we drove more than eight hundred miles to this town of about ten thousand.

The last twenty hundred and fifty to three hundred miles were on unpaved roads. We were covered with road dust and itching from mosquito bites when we finally saw the lights of Yellowknife about one a.m. Saturday. We cheered at the sight. I drove nearly the whole way, and my arms ached all day.

Sharon had root canal work started on a front tooth before we left Edmonton. It bothered her throughout the trip, but we thought most of the pain was caused by the bumpy ride.

It wasn't. The pain progressively worsened. Mike, a doctor with whom we're staying, arranged for Sharon to quickly see a dentist. He worked on her teeth twice on Sunday, and she was started on antibiotics.

This morning, she woke up with stiff and swollen jaws. Mike and the dentist operated on Sharon's mouth this evening and she will be in hospital for a few days.

We had planned to start back to Edmonton tomorrow, stopping to camp along the way. But now it looks as if we will remain here all week, until we are certain Sharon has recovered.

We also had planned to go to the Calgary Stampede and camp in the Canadian Rockies near Jasper. But now we'll have to do those things another time. The important thing is for Sharon to get well.

*****

We had rented a canoe to go fishing Sunday on the Yellowknife River. Needless to say, Sharon didn't go. I went alone and caught eight pike. I really had a good time, although I wish she could have been with me.

It was so wonderful to be in such a quiet, beautiful place, with no signs or sounds of civilization anywhere.

*****

Tonight, after making certain that Sharon was okay, I went flying with John, a surveyor, who bought a plane with Mike and another doctor. We flew all the way to the end of the road, about fifty miles. After that, there was nothing but wilderness. Yellowknife is surrounded by lakes, ponds, and desolate landscape. It's not pretty. But it is beautifully stark.

By the way, this far north this time of year, darkness doesn't descend until well after midnight, so I had plenty of light to see where civilization ends.

Mike is an ENT doctor. During the winter, he flies to remote outposts to treat Eskimos, Indians, and a few whites.

Mike and his wife, Caroline, have been good hosts. Both have good senses of humor and are easy to talk to and have fun with.

Both also are British, Mike from Surrey and Caroline from Stratford-upon-Avon. Their son, Nicholas, cried much of the time, probably because he is cutting teeth.

Mike told me about his trips to the Eskimo and Indian settlements during winter, and I think I'll be able to write a good story for the *Post* about his work. He also showed slides. They keep their mukluks, made of caribou, in the freezer during summer so they won't rot and fall apart. We had moose for dinner one night and Arctic char another.

*****

On Friday, I saw an elephant race in downtown Yellowknife. A circus was in town, and the race was a promotion. Thousands showed up to watch. I took lots of photos, including a funny one of a well-dressed woman looking disgusted as she walked past a huge pile of elephant dung.

*****

In Edmonton and before her hospitalization here, Sharon and I slept together and had sex. She said she started taking the pill—"for the first time ever"—just before I came. That "first time" can be interpreted in two entirely different ways: No sex before. Or no precautions before. I'm guessing the latter.

She made the initial move. I told her that I wouldn't have made any advances, and I wouldn't have. I'm her guest, and I wouldn't think of doing anything so presumptuous. Also, I remember her stopping my first advances when we both had too much sangria in Spain.

Sharon said I hadn't changed since we were together in Europe. I said she hadn't either. She said she was hoping she had matured.

She also said many flattering things about me: I'm the most honest person she ever has met. A part of her will die again when I leave, etc.

I'm not sure what that "honest" comment is about. I'm just me.

She said she doesn't think she ever will marry, but that is all right; she is accustomed to being alone. "I rather like it," she said.

Maybe I'm wrong, but I almost got the impression that she wanted me to suggest something permanent. I didn't.

She said she loves me. I said I love her. And I do. But I don't want to marry her or anyone else right now.

She said she doesn't want our being intimate to spoil our friendship. She said she wants us to be friends when we're fifty. I said we will be.

Tuesday, July 20, Edmonton, Alberta

We started back from Yellowknife on Sunday, after a party until nearly two a.m. Sharon and I both had too much to drink at the dentist's house, where he talked us into going with him to the annual hospital party at Great Slave Lake, which consisted of more drinking around a giant bonfire.

Sharon and I went skinny-dipping. The water felt really good, cool and refreshing, but hordes of misquotes descended when any skin showed above the surface.

We got about three hours of sleep before starting the eighteen-hour drive. I drove the unpaved roads while Sharon slept. We got to Edmonton about one thirty a.m., made love, and got about three hours of sleep before heading to the airport.

Sharon looked so sad when we said goodbye. She's such a kind, gentle person, and it really hurt to see her so mournful looking.

*****

On our trip back, we stopped in Manning, a town in Northern Alberta, to visit a priest who is a friend of Sharon's family. The priest loves hot weather and hates the cold, and he lives less than a thousand miles from the Arctic Circle. What's wrong with that picture?

He said moose come into the town during winter and have to be chased out of the street. He also said two of his parishioners were killed by bears last year.

Bears and people seem to be at war up there. Farmers keep electric fences around their beehives, but sometimes the bears get hungry enough to go right through the fences.

Black bears sit down in fields of oats, spread their legs, and scoot with their front paws as they go. Government workers trap problem grizzlies in the national parks and release them around Manning.

Oil workers and farmers carry rifles in their trucks and shoot on the move when they see bears because that way "a game warden has no idea who did it."

Friday, July 23, Flat River, Missouri

Sheila sent me a humorous book—*Real Men Don't Eat Quiche*—and a long letter. She said she hoped I missed her "shamefully."

Since the middle of June, I have travelled nearly eight thousand miles, from Miami to the Northwest Territories. I'm a little tired, but I really enjoyed myself. Old friends and new places, as well as a few new friends, make for an unbeatable combination.

*****

My brother Craig and his daughter, Monica, came down today. During supper, Dad told Craig to be sure to put a seat belt on Monica for the trip back.

Then he told about driving with me in the front seat when I was a baby. He said that when he hit the brakes, I fell out of the seat and down under the dashboard. He started laughing so hard he could barely talk. The last I heard as I left the room was him telling about how dirty the floor of the car was, Craig also laughing, and Mother saying, "I don't think that's very funny."

I didn't either. I don't remember the incident. But I remember him laughing about other things that hurt me. He has a terribly cruel sense of humor. Also, he's never given me one word of praise or encouragement for anything I've done. As an adult, I now can see that my desire for that probably played a large role in my excelling as a student and athlete, as well as always being a "good boy."

And in watching his behavior with his grandchildren, I can see that how he treated me as a child was more about him than me. For example, if my sister, Rhonda, comes in with her daughter, Emily, he might say to the child, "Oh, no, is that you again?" Of course, he would tell you that is just teasing her.

Wednesday, August 4

Sheila left today. Sadly, I was uncomfortable most of the time she was here. Of course, it didn't help that I'm living at home for the summer before moving to an apartment in St. Louis for my new teaching job.

She just doesn't seem to know how to relate to people. Any time we talked, I had to start the conversation, and then I did 90 percent of the dialogue. Her 10 percent usually was answering my questions. Also, she has a habit of saying, "Uh-huh, yeah" very softly as someone starts talking to her. I found it very distracting.

We had dinner with Roxanne and Vince in St. Louis last night. I mentioned that Sheila had met John, Roxanne's brother, the night before. Roxanne then asked if Sheila had met "little Roxanne," John's daughter.

Shelia immediately started with the "Uh-huh, yeah." But she *hadn't* met "little Roxanne." As it turned out, she thought Roxanne was talking about Brandy, the little poodle running around in Roxanne's living room.

Roxanne told me later she realized what was going on.

*****

Charlie, who went with me to the airport on Sunday to pick Sheila up, said she was nice but "I didn't understand what she was talking about."

Sheila missed her scheduled flight from Detroit to Chicago, and so she was an hour late getting into St. Louis. I made two calls to Flat River to see if she had called to leave a message, and I tried unsuccessfully to call her relatives in Detroit. I had her paged twice in the airport. Charlie and I were just getting ready to leave when she showed up.

At the airport, Shelia bought drinks. The bill was $4.20. She gave the waitress a five-dollar bill and a one-dollar bill. When the waitress brought the change back, it took a while for the two of them to figure out what to do.

All of this is not to say I don't like Sheila. I do. But there definitely can be nothing between us.

Another reason that I almost forgot: I don't think she owns a pair of cutoffs, jeans, or sneakers. At least I've never seen her in them, not even in Miami when we went fishing.

I took her to see Johnson's Shut-Ins and Elephant Rocks State Parks. She wore gold shoes with heels. She was the only person at either place who wasn't wearing sneakers or sandals. At the Shut-Ins, she wanted to try wading, so she took off her shoes. The bottom was slippery, and she fell and bruised her legs.

The outdoors obviously is not a part of her world, and it is a big part of mine.

Now I have to tell Grace about Sheila's visit. She won't be too happy, I'm afraid, since she's tried playing matchmaker for me since my divorce in 1976.

Sheila said the twins weren't friendly to her after I left. I think they will be happy to hear about her visit that was awkward at best for me and probably for her as well.

II: Veteran

Sunday, August 29, St. Louis

School starts tomorrow for teachers at Parkway North High School. Kids begin on Thursday. I'll have much more to do this year than I did at Webster Groves last year. I'll be teaching journalism and English, as well as acting as adviser for both the newspaper and yearbook. I'll also be getting paid more than $3,000 more than I was last year.

I feel very energized this time around, instead of anxious as I did last year, and am really looking forward to tomorrow. A year of experience does that, I guess. Also, part of this euphoric feeling is caused by the exercise I got today, I think. I played three softball games with Vince and Roxanne's team, and I played well.

*****

I'm living in an apartment complex less than a mile from the school in suburban St. Louis. I think I'm going to like being that close, especially since I can walk.

*****

I've had two articles published in the *St. Louis Post-Dispatch* during August, one about the Suncoast Seabird Sanctuary and another about a drunken driver incident that I witnessed while riding with a friend who is a highway patrolman.

Southern Outdoors Magazine likes my article about big river catfishing. I just sent photos to go with the piece. I should hear something on them this week.

My writer friend and mentor, Paul Hemphill, is going to stop by here at the end of September. He's going to Iowa to do a piece for *GEO* about Middle America.

*****

Rebecca is pregnant. Grace called with the news Friday. Doug and Grace want her to have an abortion. Rebecca is against it. More later when I found out what has happened.

Monday, September 6

Rebecca had an abortion. She and George are still talking about marriage. Grace said, "But it's not as serious as before."

*****

I had a long talk with my sister last night. I stopped by her house on my way back up here, intending to stay only a few minutes. I was there for more than three hours.

Rhonda and Joe are going to counseling. She found out that he had met Kathy, one of her friends, at the Farmington airport one night last summer. At first, Joe denied it. But then Rhonda confronted Kathy.

Well, actually, she did a lot more than that. She drove to Kathy's home, where she was sick in bed, and brought her back to their house to face Joe. The two told Rhonda that they "talked."

Kathy is a notorious flirt. In addition, I think she's extremely bored and unsatisfied with her life and does whatever she can to spice it up. She married on rebound about ten years ago, only two months or so after her fiancé was killed in a car wreck.

Rhonda sounded as if the counseling is helping both of them, but especially her. Much of the time, evidently, has been spent analyzing her insecurities, many of them caused by mother's smothering.

*****

Rhonda and Joe are keeping a foreign exchange student, Alexandra, from Monterrey, Mexico. The girl speaks little English, and they speak no Spanish, but I think it will be a good experience for all, especially their daughter, Emily. I speak a little Spanish, so "Allie" and I can communicate some. To welcome her,

I took her some "flores" and told her they were for her "cuarto."

*****

I have so much to do at school that it is almost overwhelming.

Wednesday, September 15

I still have much to do. But I'm getting there. I'm feeling more secure, more at home.

The teacher I replaced had a fetish for forms and paperwork. The newspaper editor told me that all she (the editor) did in journalism class was "cut and paste." In other words, paper busywork. I'm trying to cut down on having forms for everything and keeping the students busy with paste and scissors. I believe in learning by doing and not letting your life and your work be smothered in bureaucracy.

The yearbook editors told me that the former teacher wasn't liked by a lot of people and that she wasn't much fun to work with. They've indicated that they like my "low-key" attitude.

Both the newspaper and the yearbook staffs seem self-motivated. But no one on the newspaper staff has experience. And only the coeditors worked on the yearbook last year. I've been told that the former teacher allowed only seniors on the newspaper staff. I hope to change that.

Journalism is only a one-semester course here, and it is an elective, not an English course as it was at Webster. Those two facts, I think, hurt the quality and number of people taking journalism and, eventually, working on the newspaper.

I called Webster Groves today and talked to Mary, one of the girls I picked to be coeditor of the newspaper this year. I miss the students there.

I'm also teaching Sophomore English at Parkway North. I'm not overwhelmed with joy about that. No major problems so far. But one of the boys in sixth hour has a big mouth, and I might have to take measures to settle him down.

Saturday, October 9

I haven't written in too long a time. Still getting acclimated, I guess.

*****

Paul Hemphill stopped by last Saturday on his way to Iowa. He hasn't changed much since I took his writing class at Florida A&M in Tallahassee and we became good friends. But on a positive note, he said that he has quit drinking, even though he brought me a bottle of Scotch. So…we didn't drink it together.

He also gave me an autographed copy of *Too Old to Cry*, his latest book. It's another collection of his magazine and newspaper pieces. Last one didn't sell too well. But his novel about minor league baseball, *Long Gone*, did, and he's hoping it will be a movie someday.

*****

I really like Parkway North. But I'm not fond of teaching Sophomore English. Students of that age require constant structure and discipline, and several of them really don't like English. No, make that *many* of them really don't like English. I have two Sophomore English classes now. Next semester, I'll have three. Oh, joy.

Thus far, I've given one sermon to my journalism students and one to the *Norsestar* newspaper staff. Both seemed effective.

The students in journalism were talking too much. I preached to them about how they were hearing and not listening and how important it is for journalists—and students—to listen. I also moved some of them.

The *Norsestar* students were complaining about working after school every three weeks. Also, they were doing a poor job in their haste. The coup de grace came when a mother called and complained about the inconvenience that I was creating for her by requiring her daughter to stay after school. Her daughter stayed about fifteen minutes, the least of anyone.

I gave the students a choice. I pointed out the benefits they have with the present system, including no tests or reading and the freedom to come and go as long as I know what they are doing. Their only responsibilities are to meet their deadlines and work after school once every three weeks. And we celebrate birthdays.

Then I said the alternative is to work only during class, a regularly structured class with tests and no birthday parties. Guess which option they chose.

*****

One of my sophomore girls seemed genuinely shocked to learn I am younger than her mother. How depressing!

*****

Looks as if I will be the coach for the junior girls in the annual powderpuff game.

The game was cancelled last year because of fear of injuries and inappropriate behavior. The game seemed to deteriorate every year, I was told, primarily because of a lack of supervision. Big surprise there. Since boys coached the girls.

So now the game is back with faculty coaches. Lisa, my newspaper editor, asked me to do it.

*****

Social life is slow. But at least Vince and Roxanne have become my friends and I see them occasionally. We were supposed to play in a coed softball tournament this weekend, but it got rained out. If it hadn't, I wouldn't be writing this.

Sunday, October 10

Not so slow anymore!

I was just about to go to bed about eleven thirty last night when a knock came at my door. I almost didn't answer it.

The knocker was Kim, an Ozark Air Lines flight attendant, who lives across the hall from me. She asked if I'd like to come over and "have a beer."

I said, "Okay."

I figured she was having a party at her place or maybe she and her boyfriend wanted to welcome me to the area. Boy, was I wrong. She was alone.

She had been drinking, but I couldn't tell how much until we went after beer and she drove. Then it was easy to tell.

We decided on wine instead. She bought. Then came the white-knuckle drive back to her apartment. I know I shouldn't have let her get behind the wheel again. But you try having that conversation with an inebriated stranger in the parking lot of a liquor store after midnight, especially if it's her vehicle and she has the keys. At least the drive was short and traffic was light.

Kim drank heavily. It was impossible to have any sort of coherent conversation with her. But she spoke well enough that I knew she had experienced a bad night before knocking on my door. She mentioned her married boyfriend who was away in Florida and a friend in Georgia whom she had gotten mad at over the phone. Also, she had just gotten back from more than a week of flying, and only her cats were there to greet her.

First, she was subtle, smiling and singing along to records being played on her stereo. I made no move, except to leave.

Then she was more direct. She asked me to "lay" with her, "stay" with her, and "make love" to her.

I said no as gently as I could.

Then she said she was dying of cancer and didn't have much time left. Finally, she said she couldn't have children.

I escaped about two thirty a.m. after she passed out on my shoulder as I stroked her hair, my virtue still intact. Before I left, I wiped drool off her face and cat puke off her sofa. The cat might have been drinking too, although I was too busy keeping Kim at arm's length to notice.

"Why me?" I first asked myself. Then I counted my blessings. The inconvenience I suffered is insignificant compared to the torment she must feel in her life. And while I didn't satisfy her more carnal needs, I did provide her a shoulder to pass out on, while I gained a story that my guy friends would never believe—especially the part about me not sleeping with a drunk, attractive flight attendant.

Monday, October 11

Angela and Amy, two of my students from Webster, brought me a birthday cake today. It really lifted my spirits. I should have hugged them when they left.

Angela's birthday also is tomorrow. I mailed a card to her on Saturday.

Tuesday, October 25

Haven't seen or heard from Kim since that bizarre night more than two weeks ago. Really didn't think I would either.

Of course, I had never seen her before she knocked on my door either.

*****

Down in Miami, Rebecca ran away with George. They've been gone a couple of weeks. Grace doesn't know where they are, but she suspects they are living with some of George's relatives.

The first time Grace called to tell me the runaway news, she was very upset. Last night, she seemed a little more together. She and Doug seem to have had problems with Rebecca since the abortion.

I think Rebecca really resents giving in on that issue, and leaving home was her way of striking back. By phone, she told Grace that she left so she and George can save money, which probably is the opposite of what is happening.

Grace also said Linda and Felix want to move back from Orlando and live with them, probably so Grace can take care of the baby due in November. Karen, the oldest of the four girls, also wants to move back in and go back to school. I think she's twenty-two now. Yikes!

*****

Paul stopped by on his way back from Iowa. While he was here, Sharon called from Edmonton. Mike and Caroline Knowland, her friends from Yellowknife, were at her flat. They are moving to Portland, Maine, and said they might stop by here on the way. I hope so.

And speaking of Sharon's flat. It contains what I suspect is the world's smallest bathroom, even smaller than what I encountered in Europe. You have to be a contortionist to close the door after you are inside.

*****_

School goes well. But I still don't like teaching Sophomore English. I really yelled a couple of times last week. I hate doing that, but sometimes it's necessary to get them quiet. I do think, however, that gradually I am building a rapport with most of them. A few are out of reach, unfortunately.

*****

I think I have a hemorrhoid. The decline and fall of my immortality has begun. Rats! I suspect I got it because of a hard slide I did into third base during one of our coed softball games. Whatever the cause, though, it itches like crazy. Double rats!

Sunday, October 31

Hemorrhoid watch: It's better, less itchy, thank goodness. But I didn't go to school Friday, and I've spent almost all weekend lying around. Every year, it seems, I get a bad sinus infection about this time, when warm weather follows a frost. About noon today, I finally started feeling better.

TV has been broken since Wednesday night. I really missed it this weekend, but I kept busy. I read four magazines and then finished one novel and started another. In just those two books, I read about five hundred pages. I also did a couple of hours of schoolwork, paid bills, wrote a letter to Mam Ma, and cleaned my leather boots and shoes.

*****

A few weeks ago, seven people died from taking poisoned Tylenol. Since then, copycat crazies have popped up all over the country. They're putting poison, pins, and razor blades in both medicine and food. Trick or treat was called off in towns all across the country. If I had children, I wouldn't have let them go to strangers' houses. How can we do such things to each other? How can we dare call ourselves civilized?

And while I'm asking questions: will I ever have children? Having endured my father's abuse, I'm more than a little concerned I might model his behavior, even though I'd hate myself for it. And yelling at my students, as I did the other day, is a perfect example of that behavior.

I've been calling students "my kids" for a while now.

Wednesday, November 10

Rebecca and George were married Friday. Grace called and took about forty-five minutes to relate the harrowing story.

Rebecca called her on Wednesday and asked if she and Doug were busy on Friday. When Grace said they were, Rebecca replied, "It's too bad you can't come to our wedding."

She said the wedding was going to be a small one. Her twin sister Rachel was invited, but not Linda or Karen. She hung up.

On Thursday, Rebecca called Rachel and asked her to take her prom dress to George's mother. Rachel refused.

At that time, Grace still didn't know the address or home number of where Rebecca and George were staying. Linda called George's mother and got the phone number from her. Then she gave it to Grace.

Whoever was on the other end hung up on Grace several times when she tried calling on Friday morning. Eventually a voice she didn't recognize answered and, Grace said, gave her "the runaround."

Eventually, Tevia, George's uncle and the owner of the house, told Doug that they could attend the wedding but they weren't welcome. He said that they, along with Rachel, should drive to a certain phone booth and then call him again.

They followed the instructions and, a few minutes later, Tevia arrived at the phone booth in a maroon Mercedes. They followed him to the house.

It was "palatial," and dozens of cars filled the circular driveway. The girl who greeted them at the door wore a long evening gown.

Rachel was wearing jeans because she had been afraid Rebecca had nothing to wear and she didn't want to embarrass her.

People filled the house while Rebecca was behind a locked door. Grace demanded to see her, the door was unlocked, and the three of them were allowed inside.

Grace said Rebecca was wearing "silks, satin, and lace," while a woman "stoned on something" was putting flowers in Rebecca's hair. Grace dismissed all non-family members from the room.

Rebecca was happy to see them, Grace said. She added that Rebecca seemed a bit disoriented and her eyes looked as if she had been crying. They hugged her and shared their love with her.

Grace then found George, talked to him, and hugged him too. She refused to shake his father's hand.

Doug warned her to be careful because "we don't know yet how we're going to get out of here."

Rebecca and George were married. Grace said a prayer during the service, with Rebecca's consent.

Grace said she saw someone give Rebecca and George a wedding gift of $4,000 cash.

She, Doug, and Rachel left soon after the service, stopping at Burger King for supper.

By the time Grace finished with her story, I was ready for some of the scotch that Paul gave me, and I felt I had just listened to the plot for a made-for-TV movie.

*****

Powderpuff game is Friday. Thank goodness another teacher is helping me with the junior girls. I knew only four of them when practices began, and we have a fifty-five-player roster with six practice sessions.

It's been chaotic but fun. And the girls really seem to enjoy playing.

One of them said to me, "I'm a linebacker. Is that offense or defense?"

We'll probably lose.

Friday, November 12

Yes, we lost, but only 12–10. We played well—as well, that is, as fifty-five girls who never had played football before could play. We had fewer penalties than the seniors. We had no fumbles, while they had several. And we executed our plays better. We missed a second, and winning, touchdown by two yards.

The girls really seemed to enjoy the game, and so did I, despite the bitter cold.

They gave me purple sweatpants that have "Coach Montgomery, Powderpuff 82" on the front of the legs and "I heart 84" on the butt.

Everyone met in the middle of the field when the game was over and hugged one another. Feeling so good there really made me depressed, however, when

I came home to spend an evening alone. It reminded me that I really need someone to share my life with.

*****

I'm really mad at myself. As I was acting a little silly in Sophomore English the other day, one of the girls called me "queer." I mildly admonished her and told her to watch her language. Only later did I realize she had been the using the word as it was intended, to mean strange or unusual. Meanwhile, I had done exactly the same thing my mother used to do when I, as a small child, also used the word correctly.

Thursday, December 2

An assistant principal sat in on my sixth-hour class yesterday to evaluate me. Sixth hour is Sophomore English and my worst-behaved class of the day.

Students certainly were not on their best behavior either.

On the negative side: Too much talking and students not responding when I told them to be quiet. Open-ended questions and everyone answering at once. Students answering me with their backs to me. (They sit at round tables instead of desks.) And, most important, using subject matter in an attempt to gain order, instead of gaining order through my own presence.

On the positive side: Good kids. My enthusiasm and interest. My movement around the room. Calling on each student. No sense of frustration.

Ha! If he only knew!

Today I eliminated open-ended questions and demanded quiet before starting work. I asked students to face me when answering questions.

That critique was really a big help, I think, if only I can follow through.

*****

A girl in my journalism class went into the hospital for surgery a week before Thanksgiving. She told me she had a deviated septum. She came back with a nose job. I wonder how it must have felt for her to return with a changed appearance to a place full of people who know how she looked before.

*****

Yearbook students haven't been doing too well. Several of them did not meet deadlines for first draft of copy. Deadline for finished layout and copy is next Friday. Tomorrow I will tell them that those who miss one deadline will have their grades dropped a letter and those who miss two will be removed from the staff.

I'd rather have no rules and only responsible people. But I am learning you can't always get what you want, especially when it comes to teaching in general and student behavior especially.

The newspaper students, however, are, for the most part, very responsible. The only problem I've had has been with Benjy, the most talented writer on the staff. A couple of times he has handed in stories the next morning, when they were due the previous afternoon. Until this week, they always were acceptable.

This time, however, he handed in an essay-editorial instead of a news story. I rejected it and readily let him know that I was upset with him. It will be interesting to see what happens with the next deadline.

*****

AFS held a faculty auction to raise money for foreign exchange scholarships. Teachers donated cakes, pies, cookies, picnics, dinners, etc. I offered a float trip for three people. Lisa and Risa(both newspaper staff members) and Kim got it for $65.

We raised $1,200, but only about two dozen teachers participated. I was surprised.

*****

I'm terribly lonely and still not doing anything about it.

*****

While I was home for Thanksgiving, I walked through the living room with tennis balls in my hand. Mother asked what I was going to do with them. When I said "practice juggling," I heard Dad snicker. Always he has been negative, and always he will remain that way.

But at least I'm growing. I knew he would respond that way and yet I answered Mother truthfully, instead of mumbling "nothing" as I might have a few years ago.

I taught myself to juggle several years ago, by the way, when I had a severe case of mononucleosis and little else to do all day.

Sunday, December 5

I fell up and off an escalator Friday. Yeah, I know, only me.

The newspaper staff and I had gone to the Chesterfield Mall, where I took their picture with Santa for the cover of the paper. We were on our way upstairs for lunch, and I was aiming the camera down. I was totally absorbed in what I was doing when suddenly I was hurled off and onto the floor.

Nothing damaged but my ego. Everyone got a good laugh out of it, including me.

*****

We got out of school a little early Friday because of flooding on some of the streets. Parts of Missouri have gotten five to ten inches of rain this week, and rivers are supposed to be at their highest since 1973 and 1915.

Wednesday, December 15

English students have been much better behaved since I implemented the assistant principal's suggestions. Eliminating open-ended questions made a big difference, as did gaining order through my presence instead of subject matter.

*****

I yelled at journalism class on Monday. On Tuesday, I said I was sorry, but I added that it shouldn't be interpreted as an apology. I told them that they no longer hear me when I ask them to be quiet, but I demand silence when I am talking or others are asking me questions.

I then moved some people. I also said anyone asking questions from now on must speak up so the rest of class can hear. Too many of them have had a tendency to speak only to me, and the rest can't hear what they say, thus encouraging those who can't hear to make conversation of their own since they don't feel involved in whatever is being discussed.

*****

I called Webster to see why we hadn't received any issues of the *Echo*, the student newspaper there. Susan, the woman who replaced me, insisted they had been mailed.

Six to eight students then took turns on the phone talking to me. That made me feel good.

About a week later, we received three issues. The front pages look like Angela's work ("and show my influence," he added modestly). The inside pages look cluttered and unprofessional.

*****

I asked Lynne, one of the newspaper staff members, about her overdue story. She started to cry before I had even finished asking. I didn't press it but told her I was available if she wanted to talk. She's one of the most conscientious on the staff, and I imagine she already was giving herself a much harder time for missing the deadline than I ever would.

*****

First yearbook deadline was this week. I am not happy with the progress. I don't know how we would ever get it done if editors Anna and Nancy (especially Anna) weren't on the staff again this year. They are the only veterans, and they know far more than I. At

Webster, I was adviser for just the newspaper, and the yearbook is a much different animal.

*****

As I was talking down the hall today, a girl I don't know said, "There goes Anna's idol."

*****

I am increasingly restless at night. I've been channeling some of that energy into juggling. I'm getting pretty good too! Too bad *The Ed Sullivan Show* isn't on TV anymore.

1983

Tuesday, January 4

Christmas Break was uneventful. Weather was warm and rainy, so I didn't get to go cross-country skiing or ride horses with my sister. I read, wrote, played a little basketball, saw a few movies, and went to Mike's house for some poker games.

I spent New Year's Eve at my parents' home recovering from an intestinal bug. I had gotten really sick early Thursday and still was weak. I lost five pounds in two days.

*****

The days before Christmas at Parkway North were a bit much. Parties, food, carols, etc. to excess. On the plus side, students brought in literally tons of clothes for the needy in the school-wide charity drive.

It's good to be back. The first semester will be over week after next. Students seem much more at ease than they were before Christmas.

*****

My article and photos on Dr. Mike Knowland and Yellowknife ran in the *Post* last week.

A few days before, my Eskimo wall hanging arrived. It was made by one of Mike's former patients. Both she and her husband had been drinking too much, and Mike encouraged her to put her time into art instead of alcohol. It smelled of wood smoke, a nice touch of authenticity.

She charges only for materials, which is $30. Hangings similar to mine sell for several hundred dollars in Yellowknife.

Monday, January 17

I went to Flat River this past weekend. Charlie and Mike already are talking about softball. In fact, they practiced last week. I got caught up in the excitement too. It depressed me to leave them and that excitement and come back up here.

Right now, I feel as if I belong nowhere. This year, much more than last, I've grown away from Flat River, and I feel more comfortable up here on my own. But I'm so much lonelier up here. At least down there I have people to talk to—even if the only things we have in common are fishing and softball.

I'm sure that if I could just get close to someone up here, I would feel a sense of place. I'm far more at home here than I was in the duplex, where I lived last year while teaching at Webster. That place always seemed only a temporary stop.

I'm taking a fencing class. Maybe I can get to know some people that way. Class starts in early February.

I play basketball every Thursday with Vince and a few others.

By the way, Vince and Roxanne were married earlier this month.

*****

This is the last week of first semester. Starting next week, I will have three sections of Sophomore English. Yuck!

But I am handling the classes a lot better since my evaluation. I ask students to repeat what I said. I say a name and then ask a question. I insist on quiet because I am the teacher, not because there is work to be done. Instead of yelling for silence, I stand quietly and wait until I have everyone's attention.

*****

Grace has hepatitis. Also, she recently was in an auto accident, but not injured. Her life with Doug still is one big commotion.

Rebecca and George are living with them, and Karen is at home as well. Karen's boyfriend, Danny, fell out of his car and into the driveway the other day. Karen said he had too much beer and cocaine. He's big, about six-seven. Somehow they managed to drag him into the house.

Grace gave Karen a choice of calling an ambulance or his parents. She chose the latter. His family owns a cruise line, and Danny seems to be a spoiled rich kid.

*****

Tuesday, February 8

Friday night, I had my first date in many months. Her name is Cathy. She's twenty-one and recently divorced. Vince arranged it.

We're going out again this Friday night. She's interested in sharks of all things! She's also knowledgeable in many other areas. And not bad-looking. I like her.

*****

I played in a coed softball tournament with Vince and Roxanne this past weekend. It was cold and muddy, but I had a great time. Forty teams were entered in the annual charity event, and we made it to the quarterfinals. The team that won it was the team that we beat for the championship of the fall league.

I was 10 for 13 with four home runs, but one of those three outs came with us losing 4–2 in the last inning, the bases loaded, and two outs. No matter how well you do, the mistakes are what stay with you, no matter how small or few they are or how great your contributions.

*****

Southern Outdoors is going to pay my way to Arkansas to write at least three articles on fishing the Arkansas River and its impoundments. It also bought my humor essay about fish names, which I wrote during Christmas break. No other sales, but I still have a few queries and articles out.

*****

English classes seem to be going well. Newspaper class is okay too. But I'm unhappy with yearbook people. A week ago Friday, two of the staff members and I stayed until eight p.m. to meet deadline, and I see the same thing developing again.

Also, I've been too crabby with the class lately, probably because I'm frustrated with several of them. Tomorrow I clear the air. I don't like myself when I'm crabby and pushy, and I'm not going to behave that way. Either they do the work and get good grades or they don't. It's up to them. I hope, however, that I can motivate them by explaining my feelings and frustrations and appealing to their senses of pride and responsibility.

*****

My fencing class starts tomorrow night. Yay! Athos, Porthos, Aramis, and D'Artagnan, make way for a fifth musketeer!

*****

Still no significant snow. Robins are back. Cardinals—not the baseball kind—are singing.

Monday, February 21

Winter really seems gone. Temperature was 72 degrees yesterday and nearly that again today. Trees will be green in early March if this continues. I can't remember another winter this mild.

*****

Just returned from Flat River. We had a three-day weekend. God, how the time flies. It seems as if I was just leaving on Friday. I still look forward to Fridays and "going home," the same way I did in college. Will I ever grow up? Will I ever have a home anywhere besides Flat River?

*****

My father goes to the doctor tomorrow. He might have to be hospitalized for tests and observation. He has been having some discomfort in his chest. He also is drinking quite a bit of alcohol again, especially on weekends. He smokes, although it's a pipe now instead of cigarettes. And he's overweight again.

It's like he doesn't seem to care about that heart attack he had in 1979 and what the doctor told him to do and not do in the wake of it. And, honestly, I suspect maybe he doesn't. He's always seemed to be a depressed and unhappy man, mostly laughing only at the expense of others.

*****

Craig, who is eight years younger than I, was hospitalized for tests the week before last. As he was leaving his job as a security guard at a hospital, he became ill. He doctor feared an ulcer, but test results were negative. Craig evidently has a severe case of gastritis. As a hospital employee, his stay and care are free, thank goodness.

*****

The workout at my second fencing class was incredible. We exercised for more than an hour. I liked it, although I suspect many did not. This class really should get me in shape.

Alas, it's no way to meet women, though. The class has twelve men and one woman. The instructor said the sex split is usually "about even." Just my luck that it isn't this time.

*****

I've gone out with Cathy twice. Hope to see her again. But she hasn't been home the last three times I've called. I left my phone number tonight so she can call me. It will be interesting to see if she does.

*****

Sharon sent me a cassette recording of flute music by Zamfir. It's beautiful! I'm going to take it to school to play during my planning period.

*****

We had our first preseason softball game Saturday. What did Man have before baseball/softball to keep him going through the winter? What did he have to look forward to? I love the shared anticipation.

*****

Classes continue to be all right. We now have mailed in eighty-eight of two hundred and four yearbook pages. For a while, I tried riding a few of the procrastinators pretty hard. All that did was make me mad at them and, even worse, make me dislike myself.

So I gave a sermon. I told them that I didn't like the yearbook class very much at the moment. It was a variation on the speech that I gave to the newspaper staff early in the school year. I mentioned how little they really had to do compared to some of their other classes and yet how they neglected doing it well and on time. I also told them I didn't like myself for the way I had treated a few of them and that I was going to stop it.

"No more riding and no more harassing," I said. "Instead, I'll give good grades for good work and bad grades for bad, and those who pick up the slack will be rewarded the most."

A few days later, we worked until seven p.m. on the day of deadline, and one girl still didn't finish. I knew she wouldn't. She had been one of those I was riding. Not once, however, did I say, "I told you so." On the other hand, she did a lot of blaming herself, and I didn't stop her.

With the next deadline, March 23, we'll see if she learned her lesson.

*****

A couple of weeks ago at South Junior, a boy shot and killed a student and wounded another. He then put the pistol to his head and killed himself. He carried the gun, ammunition, and a sheath knife into school in a gym bag. The two he shot supposedly had been making fun of his older brother.

The boy left a three-page suicide note, but its contents haven't been revealed.

The second aspect of the incident is that something like it could have occurred—and still could—at North or any other Parkway school or any school anywhere. The best way for tragedies like that to be prevented is for people to be a whole lot kinder than they probably are capable of being. The more practical solution, I guess, is to turn our schools into armed camps, with security checks at the doors and armed guards.

*****

Cathy just returned my call. We're going out again—Friday, March 4. She's busy this coming weekend. I'm going to have to find someone else to date in addition. A date once every three weeks simply is not enough.

Monday, February 28

M*A*S*H., the best television series of all time, ended tonight. It ran for eleven years. Its conclusion severed one more tie to my youth. *M*A*S*H.*, the movie, was released during my senior year in college. Now it is over and my life goes on. I'm saddened both by the loss of a quality program and by the progression it marks in my life.

CBS local news now is showing a "behind the scenes" look at the last episode and providing coverage of area "*M*A*S*H.* bashes." I chose not to watch. I don't want to know how the sausage is made. I just want to enjoy the sausage. I want the escapism and entertainment that TV programs and movies provide, not a reminder that none of it is real.

*****

The assistant principal gave me a copy of my yearly evaluation. It is really good. But I'm not happy with my performance, especially with the yearbook staff. Next year, I will be better.

Sunday, March 13

My niece, Emily, left a note to God on her dresser. It read, "Dear God, please give me mumps, a 107-degree temperature, vomiting, and diarrhea."

Mom told Rhonda that she probably did it because she remembered when she was sick last year and Rhonda stayed home with her and "gave her all the attention."

I said the note probably had something to do with school. Mom said, "But she makes good grades," as if grades were the only consideration.

Rhonda really should talk to Emily's teacher. But I doubt she will.

*****

My parents have a pink, padded seat and lid on their toilet. When you get up, the lid hits you in the back. For men, urinating requires two hands for protection and direction. I asked Mom if she "test drove" the seat before buying it. She said she didn't like it either, but my aunt gave it to them.

"When somebody gives you something like that, you have to use it," Mom said.

Of course you do. You have to in case the person who gave it to you stops by sometimes. I'm glad my aunt didn't give them a nuclear missile.

*****

A black woman insists Parkway North is racist, and she got a local newspaper to print her opinions as a news story. The reporter didn't bother to try to verify anything, and she admitted it. Many people at North are upset, including me.

Of course, I'm upset because of the shoddy journalism. The black woman certainly is entitled to her opinion. But when one-sided opinions appear in news space, they are viewed as facts, not opinions. Our school paper is going to print an editorial criticizing the piece, along with an analysis of what was wrong with it, and an article voicing the opinions of black students at North.

The administration is understandably nervous about this woman. Officials have decided to keep a low profile instead of counter-attacking. Parkway, I'm certain, could win a libel suit against the woman, the reporter, and the paper. But St. Louis County's desegregation of schools by busing is a hot issue now. Publicity about this now could only hurt the Parkway district's reputation, although the whole controversy is based on the opinion of one crazy lady.

Understandably, the principal is nervous about what we are going to print. But he made no attempt to censor us, which would get the school in even more trouble. I sympathize with his predicament, especially after he showed me a letter from the woman. She said she would hold him responsible if any harm was done to her daughter because the article was read to North students. She implied that he authorized the reading, although he did not.

Yes, I sympathize, but our paper is obligated to present an accurate account of what has happened—at least in terms of the unprofessional journalism and its consequences.

The principal said the offending newspaper called him and volunteered to do "our side of the story," complete with photos. He refused. But he told me, "The paper will be covering school activities more fully in the future."

My fifth-hour English class wrote a letter to the editor of the paper. I doubt it gets printed, but I certainly hope it does.

The woman accused the school of being racist because her daughter didn't play much on the basketball team. Earlier in the year, she accused an English teacher of racism because the teacher criticized her daughter. She has attempted, unsuccessfully, to get other back students to join her cause.

Only a small percentage of students living in North's attendance area are black or of other minorities. I have several in classes, and they are all good students. In the months I've been here, I've never heard the slightest complaint about prejudice by or against anyone of any skin color.

Monday, March 28, Flat River

Spring break. Weather is rotten again this year—windy, cloudy. But it's supposed to improve.

Charlie stopped by today. He's getting a divorce. Already he's eager to chase women. He has shaved off his seven-year-old beard. Putting a patch over his bad eye might help with the ladies too. But that's none of my business.

Another softball friend from down here also is getting a divorce, courtesy of his wife. He lives in the city. Right after she learned she was pregnant, she came home to her parents and refused to talk to him. The two families got into a fight over the furniture. His father suffered a broken ankle in the scuffle. Both families now are suing and countersuing. I'm certain this story has some juicy details as background.

*****

We will all get a 15 percent pay raise at Parkway North. Also, I will get more for working with the newspaper and yearbook. I am supposedly on the rehire list. I sure hope so.

I recently heard that the woman I filled in for last year at Webster Groves while she was on maternity leave is quitting. She evidently went back for one year so she could qualify for retirement pay. Although I think I like Parkway North more than Webster and she had every right to do what she did, I still feel both depressed and angry about that.

*****

Same old story. Yearbook students did not do a good job of meeting March 23 deadline. Now I get to see how my latest tactic works. I didn't ride or pressure them. I told them they were solely responsible for getting their work in on time and, if they didn't, then grades would suffer. I'm giving several Cs and Ds for third-quarter grades.

I hope this will give the slackards a little more incentive for next time. If this doesn't work, I'll have to try something else, I guess. I'm still looking for the magic formula for motivation.

I don't have this kind of problem at all with the newspaper. The reasons for the difference, I'm sure, are many.

While we were working late on March 23, Anna, one of the editors, told me that she and Mimi, one of the newspaper staffers, had come to the conclusion, independently of each other, that I am the type man they would like to marry—if only they were a little older or I was a little younger. I feel much the same way.

Why can't I find anyone nearer my own age to feel that way about?

And, no, I never will be involved in an inappropriate relationship with a student. For me, teaching isn't just about presenting information and motivating students to do well in a subject area; it's also about being a trusted authority figure and role model.

What type of man am I anyway? I should have asked, I guess. But I was too embarrassed by the compliment.

When Lois and I were in counseling before our divorce, we took the Myers-Briggs personality test. I'm an INFP, which is all the warm, fuzzy stuff. I was told that fewer than 1 percent of men are that. I don't remember what Lois's was. Counselor said we were very different people and that we'd have to work hard to make the relationship work. We chose not to.

*****

Norsestar came out Thursday with the articles criticizing the *West County Journal* for its unprofessional handling of racism charges against Parkway North. Only it isn't the *West County Journal*.

One of the assistant principals immediately called to tell me how good the articles are. But the paper hasn't been called that for a while, he added. It is the *West County Press-Journal*.

When a paper does something brave (or stupid) the way we did with another piece, the critics are eager to jump on you, the same way we jumped on the *Journal*. Several of the teachers accused us of being unprofessional for running a satire that, they thought, made fun of old people. At least we've got a week to cool off.

On Tuesday, April 5, we will sell our April Fool's edition. It's called the *National Norsestar*. More problems?

Lisa, the editor, won a Quill & Scroll national award for a sports story about how wrestlers struggle with losing weight. I entered her in the competition. Thirty-two winners were declared in that category. But hers was tops. She received a gold pin and a plaque and now is eligible for a scholarship. The school also received a plaque. There were five hundred winners in eight categories with more than thirty-five hundred entries.

*****

The faculty beat the senior boys in a basketball game. It wasn't very well organized, but still it was fun. I shot only once from the field and scored four points.

*****

Also on April 5, we're having a "fund run" to raise money for scholarships. Teachers and Honor Society members have gotten students to pledge money for number of laps run around the track. I've collected about $50 in pledges so far.

I put a twenty-lap limit on my run so students would have an idea about how much they would have to pay. Each lap is worth a nickel. A lot of them seem to think I'll be lucky to run one lap. They're in for a big surprise.

Of course, students think anyone over twenty-one is ready for a wheelchair.

Saturday, April 9, St. Louis

Fourth straight weekend of rain. Also, two solid weeks of clouds and cold. Severe flooding in many places, especially to the south. All this dreary weather makes for a lot of dreary and bored people. I feel like a caged animal. I had more or less reconciled myself to being indoors this weekend, with the hope I could at least watch some of the Cardinals games on TV. But the game last night in New York was rained out! And the one today was preempted by a hockey game!

Craig and I went to Wednesday night's game at Busch Stadium. As we drove in, radio announcers assured us the game would be played. But it was raining when we got there, and it didn't stop. Rats!

"Fund run" also was postponed. No new date yet for it.

*****

I received a letter saying that I will be rehired. I found out yesterday that I will teach Freshman English instead of Sophomore. Arrgh! Maybe I can switch with someone.

*****

Southern Outdoors has assigned me another article. I sold my first piece over the transom to that publication during spring of 1982, and the editor says he really likes my work. In fact, he even said he's afraid my writing "might be too good" for his readers.

This article will be about sportsman ethics and will be the lead article in the February issue.

*****

In Miami, Grace still is recovering from hepatitis. Rebecca and George are living in an apartment. Karen is working and going to school. Rachel is trying to break up with her boyfriend, who also dates a married woman, who just happens to be married to a pharmacist with whom Doug works. Gotta love the drama, but I'm so glad I'm no longer in the midst of it.

Meanwhile, Linda and the baby (Andrew) are living with Doug and Grace. Linda has enrolled at the University of Miami.

Grace called last night to tell me that Felix announced he doesn't want Linda to go to school and he doesn't like their baby and he doesn't want the baby. Then he went home to his parents.

I called Linda this morning and we talked for about forty-five minutes. We've had a connection since I first became friends with her family in 1976 and she was fifteen or sixteen. It's been strictly platonic. We just seem to get along well together. She mentioned coming up to see me. But I doubt she will.

Wednesday, April 13

Still raining. But we got the "fund run" in yesterday. I ran twenty-four laps (six miles) but told students they don't have to pay for more than twenty. Still, some are paying for all twenty-four. Some expressed shock, amazement, and disbelief that such an old guy could run so far. Fortunately, I had witnesses! I loved it! Surprisingly few of the teachers participated.

*****

Lisa seems really inspired by her award. She's applying for several scholarships. Winning seemed be some sort of confirmation that she has talent. I'm so happy for her.

*****

I gave some low grades to *Saga* staffers for third quarter. Several have talked to me about their grades, and today a mother called me. I hate giving grades.

But since I have to, I will give them honestly, and that includes low grades when they are merited.

*****

I must pick five students to receive awards for outstanding work in journalism. I can pick three or six or seven. But five will be tough.

*****

North County High School, near Flat River, wants to hire me. That's the only school in the area that I would work for. I had a great experience there with my student teaching. But I think I'll stay here. Drat! Why do I have to make decisions like that?

*****

I've sold short articles recently to *Southern Outdoors* and *Sports Afield*. I still have several others out. *Missouri Life* is holding my Mark Twain article for publication this summer or fall. It's a fictional piece about what the author would think of his hometown of Hannibal today.

Monday, April 18

Grace just called.

Felix just left Linda. He moved into an apartment by himself. Linda is talking about divorce.

Rachel was held hostage for a day by the guy she broke up with. He now is making a pest of himself by phoning constantly.

The next one is a dandy. A cable TV company tore up the Mayfields' front yard and driveway. Suddenly, water was several inches deep in the house. A plumber charged $195 to clean out the gutters and another $80 went for carpet cleaning. Then the flooding returned.

A second plumber discovered that the cable TV company broke a sewer line. A foreman for the company inspected the damage and promised to take care of it.

In came Action Carpet Cleaners. The company's large, fire engine-type hose exploded in the living room, sending a white chemical mist everywhere.

Through a series of phone calls, Doug managed to learn that the chemical cleaner contained several potentially dangerous ingredients. Thus far, a few headaches seem to be the only side effects, thank goodness.

Now the cable TV company has had the carpeting removed and is having it cleaned outside the house. Whew!

Right after this, a Cuban woman approached Grace at a garage sale and asked to read her palm. Grace said, "No, thanks. I'd rather be surprised."

Grace's phone calls are entertaining but also exhausting. It's like I'm experiencing what she is describing.

*****

We had several inches of snow yesterday. Temperatures are twenty degrees below normal.

Wednesday, April 27

I've been depressed for several days now, and have tried my best to figure out why. Part of it is the bad cold and/or virus that I have been fighting. Another part is the letter I got from Sharon.

I told her what Anna said about me being the type of man whom she would like to marry. Sharon put a p.s. on her letter: "I agree with the yearbook editor."

Sharon, I'm sure, would marry me. But I don't want to marry her, even though there is much about her that I admire and desire in a woman. For example, she is gentle, generous, and adventurous. She likes the outdoors.

Her p.s. depressed me because I care about her and I know she is lonely, just as I am. But I don't care enough to propose marriage. And it depresses me, I think, because I have such a low self-image, and I feel unworthy when people say such nice things to me.

Perhaps I'm depressed, too, because telling her what Anna said was a selfish and thoughtless thing to do.

Another contributor to my depression came to me as I was driving home in the rain. It's spring, a time for new beginnings, a time to start thinking about moving on—and I'm going to be here, in the same place, again next year. Compounding that realization is a Jimmy Buffett song that I have been playing daily, not realizing its effect, knowing only that I like it.

The song is "Somewhere over China," and it begins: "Just a semi-normal person, thought he had his future planned. Then he won some silly sweepstakes and he had a hundred grand. Never stopped to think of taxes. He was gone before they knew. With a flair for old romantics, to the Orient he flew. Now he's somewhere over China . . ."

I've had a couple of "Somewhere Over China" adventures in my life: when I went to Europe alone in 1976, which is where I met Sharon, and last year when I flew to Edmonton, Alberta, and we drove to Yellowknife. Also, my life has been in mostly a state of flux since my divorce in '76. No, actually it's pretty much been that way all my life. As a child, I went to eight schools, including three high schools.

And now, even though I love my job and my students, the gypsy in me is saying it's time to move on.

Friday, May 6

Felix tried to abduct Andrew, Linda's son, from the Mayfields' house. Linda threw herself in front of his car. Felix finally calmed down and Linda went for a ride with him, the baby in the back seat. Eventually he took them back home. Felix, I truly believe, is a dangerously unstable person.

He was filled with remorse after the incident, begging for sympathy and forgiveness.

Grace wants me to call Linda, but not tell her that I know what happened. She thinks Linda needs someone to talk to outside the family. But she's afraid Linda will get mad at her for meddling if she finds out that she (Grace) called me.

*****

I received proof today that the world is, indeed, a small place. Some time ago, I had heard John, another English teacher, talk about a woman with whom he had been living several years ago when suddenly she decided to marry another man. Today over lunch, he talked some more.

The woman also was a teacher at North, a business teacher. And she is a woman whom I've thought about off and on for fifteen years! Mary is her name, and we went to Mineral Area College together.

We also had the leads in two plays together, and I had a big crush on her but was too shy to let her know that I liked her. In fact, I was supposed to kiss her passionately in one scene but was too much of a wimp to do it properly. In rehearsals, I remember hoping the director would tell me to do it again and keep doing it until I got it right.

John said she now is divorced and teaching at an area business school. And I can't help but wonder… But, no, I'm not going to follow up.

*****

Norsestar staff and I went to a journalism conference at Florissant Valley College on Thursday. Webster Groves staff was there too. Webster students sought me out all day and told me how much they miss me. It really made me feel good—and bad.

Five North students won awards in writing and layout competition. Webster students won more, finishing third overall.

We also received word of ratings by the MIPA. *Norsestar* and *Webster Echo* both earned First Honors. *Echo* earned All-Missouri last year, when I was at Webster, and *Norsestar* Second Honors. So the former got worse and the latter improved. I don't know how much credit I should take for *Echo* success last year and *Norsestar* improvement this year. But at least a little, I guess.

Friday, May 13

Felix is back with Linda. They will move into an apartment soon. Grace is not happy. Tune in tomorrow for another gripping episode of this soap opera.

*****

The father of a student at North committed suicide last Sunday. He hung himself a day after his divorce became final. The wife found him and made her children come in to see the body.

One of our teachers, who also is a preacher, told all of his classes about the death from "self-inflicted" injuries. I'm still trying to figure out why he would make such an announcement.

The student didn't come to school all week. One of her friends told me that the girl's little brother is afraid to go back to school.

Saturday, May 21

Journalism picnic is supposed to be tomorrow. Torrential rains just began.

*****

One of my students ran away from home last week.

Even before I got to know her, I could tell by her eyes that she had a hard life. Then, little by little, I learned she had been emotionally, physically, and even sexually abused.

She comes across to many of the other students as a tough "burnout." But I know otherwise. From the way she talks, I can tell she has the soul of a writer. She's afraid, not tough.

She called Wednesday, and we talked for about a half hour. In good conscience, I couldn't tell her to go back home. Her mother has been married several times and now is living with a man who, according to this child, hits her anytime her mother tells him to. Evidently the mother is very unstable and now has threatened to send the girl to a detention home.

While I didn't tell her to go back home, I did say that I am afraid she will keep running away from everything for the rest of her life if she doesn't watch it.

Along with having problems at home, she is failing every class but mine, which I didn't know until she told me. Also, she talked about other kids not liking her. So, she's run away, dropped out, and is living with friends.

She says she will return to school next year. I doubt it. But I hope so.

*****

One of my students fixed me up with her boss. The date turned out well—for me, at least. I'm going to ask her out again. Her name is Cathy.

I doubt I'll ask Vince's Cathy out again. After five dates, I tried to kiss her good night. She turned her cheek to me.

I respect the fact that she is recently divorced. But after five dates, I am beginning to feel a little frustrated. I definitely do not want a platonic relationship with her.

*****

On Thursday, a bomb exploded at nearby Pattonville High School. The explosion followed a phone threat and a search that revealed nothing. Fortunately, no one was hurt. Four students were arrested the next day.

Also the next day, we got a bomb threat at nine thirty a.m. We kept the students outside until about one p.m. while the school was searched by teachers, police, and dogs. I helped search the English Department.

It was a strange experience. The whole sequence of events simply didn't seem real. I never really felt afraid, although common sense suggests I should have.

To help keep the students occupied out in the bleachers, *Norsestar* staff gave away the newspaper that we had intended to sell that day. After a few brief readings, the papers made great airplanes.

By noon, students were playing ball, polishing cars, throwing Frisbees, sunbathing, and who knows what else. It was like a '60s "happening."

No bomb was found. But I wouldn't be surprised if another threat were phoned in next week. Kids had too much fun.

Monday, May 23

The girl who ran away from home was back in school today. I haven't had a chance to talk to her.

*****

Saga and *Norsestar* students gave me a shirt, shorts, and a gift certificate at the journalism picnic.

Wednesday, June 1

No more bomb threats. But someone tried to burn down the school last night. Industrial Education Department was badly damaged. Other areas had smoke and water damage. Seventy-five people worked all night to clean up. A smoky smell was all over the building today, and most everything was covered in a film of ash.

Our final newspaper was to have been published in Industrial Education. Today I called around all day, trying to make arrangements to get it printed elsewhere. It looks as if we'll make it, but paper might not be ready until Monday, the day of graduation, instead of Friday.

*****

The school nurse donated $75 to help cover our loss when we gave the last issue away. How nice is that?

*****

The girl who ran away returned home and to her part-time job, as well as to school. I told her that I'm proud of her.

*****

On my way back from Flat River last night, I narrowly missed hitting a man on the highway. He was in the right lane, walking into traffic, instead of on the shoulder, and he was wearing dark clothes. If he wasn't drunk, he was crazy or had a death wish.

*****

While I was doing some gardening at my parents' house Monday, Mom came out and started her special way of irritating me: Why did I plant beans if I wasn't going to plant more than that? Why didn't I plant a row right there? And on and on ad nauseum.

When she asked if the gloves I was wearing "aren't your good ones," I gave my special exasperated "No!"

She became very indignant and asked self-righteously if she was doing something to "irritate" me. When I said yes, she said, "Well, I sure would like to know what it is." She was certain she had done no wrong. She never does. The other person always is the one with the problem.

So I told her—and myself, I guess. I told her that by asking that last question, she was saying that I don't have sense enough to know which gloves to use when I work in the garden. And that, I think, typifies a lot of our other exchanges. I didn't tell her that, but I think she got the point. She didn't say another word.

*****

Also at the house, someone retied the dogwood tree after I had pruned it and tied the main branches so they would grow up instead of out. Again, that was typical.

I know one thing: If I ever have children, I will allow them to grow up, to do and think for themselves. I won't remake their beds or retie their trees, or ask so many condescending questions, especially when they are adults. Different is not necessarily wrong. It simply is different. And when they reach the age of thirty-four, they should be able to tell which gloves are the "good ones," I think.

Sunday, June 12

School was out Thursday. Graduation occurred on Monday and, once more, some sick person, or persons, was at work. The school received a phone call saying that s sniper would shoot at the seniors. Police were all over, and helicopters above, but no announcement was made about the threat.

Still no one has been arrested for the fire.

*****

Two of my newspaper students won the Six Flags writing contest. First prize was $500 and tickets for the staff.

Back in April, Mimi, Lynne, and I attended Press Day at Six Flags, along with several hundred other students and advisers. Each school, then, was to submit one story about the park in general: new rides, Senior Night, kayak races, or any combination of those topics. Since content was the most important ingredient and the story wasn't due until a couple of weeks after Thunder River—the most important new ride for the article—opened, I suggested that Lynne and Mimi call the park to get information about the ride's popularity and talk to students who had tried it.

Professional journalists graded the articles, and we were told that one of the judges gave our article 100/100.

I told the staff that we could spend up to $100 of the prize for a party. But since school is now out, I doubt there will be one.

*****

Anna came in on Thursday and finished layouts on prom, graduation, and baccalaureate. I don't know how we will get a yearbook out next year without her.

Books are supposed to be delivered on August 6. But I don't think they will be on time.

*****

I've started summer school at the University of Missouri–St. Louis. I attend Tuesday and Thursday nights from five thirty to eight. The course is Problems of Teaching Reading in the Secondary School. Yuck.

But I have to take the course to get my permanent teaching certificate. At least there are quite a few good-looking women in the class to keep my attention.

The worst thing about the class is the timing. Our Flat River softball team plays at the same time, and we're doing well (6–3). We've just beaten two of the best teams. We play the third one on Tuesday, but I'll have to miss that game.

*****

I leave for Arkansas on June 20, courtesy of *Southern Outdoors*. I'm really looking forward to the trip.

I received word a week ago Friday that the magazine would buy another of my back-of-the-book essays and two short articles.

Cathy No. 2 (who lives across the street from my apartment complex) and I celebrated with an expensive dinner.

We don't have a lot in common, but I like her. She's attractive, intelligent, and has a good sense of humor.

*****

Southern Outdoors has arranged for another trip for me in August. The Bass Anglers Sportsman's Society (B.A.S.S.), the parent company, is holding its annual Bassmaster Classic, and I've been invited to attend as a press angler. The trip includes free plane tickets, lodging, and meals. I also was asked several of my clothing sizes, so I guess there will be a lot of freebies.

We will be staying in Cincinnati. But the lake where we will be fishing is being kept a secret.

*****

Sharon is coming to visit sometime in July. She will stop by here on her way to visit Michael and Caroline in Maine.

Dave and Shirley will be coming to St. Louis soon too. Although they now live in Florida, they're from this area originally.

Monday, June 27

The Arkansas trip went well. I got three stories for *Southern Outdoors* and a feature for the *Post-Dispatch*. I learned that George Washington Carver was born in Southwest Missouri, and I visited a monument to him near Diamond. Carver Day down there will be July 10, and I am pegging the story to that.

I've a lot of writing to do during the next month. It's both a good and bad prospect, mostly good.

*****

Cathy No. 2 and I went to The Muny outdoor theater last night. I'm very much attracted to her, and I think the feeling is mutual.

*****

Emily broke her arm a few weeks ago. She was eight years old on Sunday.

*****

Dave and Shirley are in St. Louis. We will get together soon. Dave said my ex still is in Tampa, working for a public relations firm. Her name now is Lois Langley.

Tuesday, July 5

Cathy and I went with Dave and Shirley to see the comedian Gallagher at the Fox Theatre Sunday night. He's the guy who breaks watermelons with a sledgehammer.

Cathy seemed edgy some of the time, especially when any mention was made of her daughter, Nicole.

She said good night to me at her door, saying she had a "big day tomorrow. My girlfriend has a picnic or something planned." I was hurt but didn't say anything.

Now I don't know whether to call her gain. Her excuse for keeping me outside was flimsy at best. But was she trying to give me the brush-off, or was she troubled by her ex-husband and daughter and didn't want to admit she was upset?

She had Nicole during all of June. But her ex took the girl on Friday or Saturday. Also, he refuses to tell her where he is going to put Nicole in school. So maybe all of that was bothering her. Or maybe not.

Maybe she just doesn't want to see too much of me and was trying to let me know. That would have been the first time that she and I had been in her apartment without Nicole.

I took Cathy and Nicole for a hamburger and to see *Superman III* last Wednesday. I felt a little uncomfortable throughout, but it got worse back at Cathy's apartment. After Nicole and I read a book together, Cathy took her to bed. About ten minutes later, she came back into the living room and said she would have to stay with Nicole, indicating that I should leave.

So what do I do? I know Cathy is having a tough time. By calling her would I complicate things for her or help her by providing companionship? I guess maybe I should ask her that question.

*****

Dave, Shirley, and I played tourists on Friday. We went to Shaw's Gardens, the Arch, Laclede's Landing, and then the West End for dinner.

*****

The float trip with the girls from North is scheduled for July 20.

Sunday, July 24

Float trip went well.

I was worried about guys on the river yelling at the girls, since they're all attractive. But it didn't happen.

The only one who got yelled at was me! A girl with a beer in her hand screamed, "Hey you, in the red shorts!" as we passed. "Nice legs!"

Cathy was going with us but then said she couldn't. She flew to Chicago on Wednesday evening to see her grandmother who was in from Florida and is staying until Monday. Because of getting Thursday–Saturday off, she said she couldn't get off on Wednesday, the day of the trip.

We went to dinner and a movie Monday night. Again, she said good night at the door. Don't know if I'll go out with her again.

I'm trying to be understanding about the complications in her life, but I'm getting little out of the relationship, and I have no incentive to continue it.

*****

Sharon arrives from Canada tomorrow for a few days.

*****

Linda is getting a divorce from Felix. We talked tonight for about forty-five minutes. She might come up for a visit. I really hope she does.

*****

While driving home from a softball game Friday night, I heard *Dateline* on KMOX radio. People call in to tell about themselves and what they're looking for in the way of dates. Listeners then call the station to get the phone numbers of people they're interested in.

I worked up my courage and called to get the number for Marsha, a twenty-eight-year-old woman who is a district sales manager and interested in sports. She's a five-seven blonde, and she sounded very energetic and full of life. But will I call her? Probably not.

*****

Southern Outdoors ran my catfish article and essay on fish names in its August issue. I got a hate letter concerning the essay. The writer said it was "much to do about nothing," among other things. I can't imagine someone getting so angry over a humor essay. The guy seemed to take it as a personal affront against the South, since that's where fish species have the most nicknames.

*****

School starts in a little more than three weeks. Where did the summer go?

Tuesday, August 2, Cincinnati, Ohio

I'm at the Bassmaster Classic.

Last night, we—competitors and press—were taken by horse-drawn carriage to a party at the Playboy Club. Some of us attended seminars today, while the rest fished the Ohio River. Those who stayed in today go out tomorrow.

Competition starts Thursday for the $40,000 first prize. Press angler who catches the largest bass each day wins $500 for himself and the contender he was with. Tomorrow I fish with Al Williams, the only black man in the tournament. Don't know yet who I will fish with when I go out again on Friday.

We've received free caps, shirts, jackets, belt buckles, duffel bags, life vests, and more. Plus, all of our meals, lodging, and transportation are taken care of. All facets, thus far, have been first class.

But is this what fishing is supposed to be? More accurately, is this what it is supposed to be for me?

I'll finally get to meet Dave Precht, the editor of *Southern Outdoors*. He is supposed to arrive tomorrow.

My roommate is Charlie Farmer, an outdoor writer from Ozark, Missouri. He has introduced me to other people.

*****

Sharon's stay was hectic. We went to the Arch, a Cards' game, Ste. Genevieve, Elephant Rocks, and Johnson's Shut-Ins.

No sex. She was off the pill. I was relieved. It's difficult for me to be intimate with a woman whom I see only once a year, even though we write often to one another.

The night before she left, Sharon said, "I don't think you know how much I love you."

I do know, and I'm uncomfortable with it. I love Sharon, but as a close, dear friend, not as a woman I want to marry.

Saturday, August 20, St. Louis

Cincinnati trip was fun, especially dinner at the Playboy Club. At my table, Bunny Carol catered to our every need. I made sure to score some Playboy Club matches.

Oh, yeah, there was fishing too, but no one caught much in the Ohio River. Biggest bass was two-eleven.

Dave Precht, the man who gave my writing career a jump start, is a quiet, unassuming man. We talked about the ethics story I wrote for *Southern Outdoors*. I worked hard on the piece, finishing up last week.

Classic next year is at Niagara Falls. I hope I'm invited.

*****

Yearbooks were handed out last week. They look good. Weakest aspect is the cover. Binding is white, instead of gray, as we requested.

A couple of the girls got a little crazy in my book. One said I have a "nice ass." Another wrote that the girls "drooled over your body all year."

Staff members were excited about the book. That made me feel good.

*****

My sister-in-law, Judy, is pregnant. Baby is due in April. She's in hospital now being treated for dehydration.

Vince and Roxanne had their baby, a girl named Samantha, just before I left for Cincinnati.

*****

I dread another year in this apartment. I want a yard and a garden where I can sweat, get my hands dirty, make things grow, and forget about the rest of the world. Next year, for sure.

Tuesday, August 30

My article on Mark Twain's return to Hannibal ran in the August issue of *Missouri Life*. Larry West, another English teacher at North, told me that he read it and said it was "beautiful." That really gave me a lift.

*****

This is our first full week of school, and I'm still enjoying the honeymoon period with my classes, including Freshman English. I really like my journalism class. It's large and could get noisy, but the kids are good ones.

Norsestar staff looks good too. I don't know about *Saga* staff yet, but I have a positive feeling. I'm worried about photography, however, because we have little darkroom experience.

*****

After not seeing her for more than a month, Cathy and I had dinner last Thursday. Guess I'll call her again. But it is not a very hot relationship.

Friday, September 9

School goes well.

But still…I have this fear that maybe I'm being too nice. I feel very relaxed this year, even with the freshmen. Maybe part of it is that I'm finally getting to enjoy a second year in the same place. I don't think I'll ever yell again.

But don't hold me to that.

The way I'm feeling now, though, is that there's simply no need to yell. Still that laid-back feeling bothers me. Maybe I don't want it to be easy.

The closest I've come to getting mad was this morning when about half the yearbook staff (five of eleven) came in late first hour. I told them that a bad habit was developing and it would have to stop. In general, however, I think the staff has more good workers this year, although I doubt any will be as good as Anna. It will take some time to find out for sure.

We have about forty black students from the city attending North this year as part of the voluntary desegregation plan. Most of them are freshmen.

The ones I have in class seem to be good students who are eager to learn and eager to please. At least one of the forty, however, transferred back to a city school. The change was too much for her, I guess.

We have had no incidents of any kind. Everyone seems to get along well.

*****

Dave Precht said my ethics article is "excellent." I'm getting paid $700 for it.

*****

Robbie called recently from New York City. He's doing really well, selling articles to newspaper and magazines, as well as running his own company, Vorhaus Communications, with his girlfriend. He's even selling stuff to *Cosmo*. Oh, yeah, he's also working for Dan Rather at CBS. Quite a success story.

Just a few years ago, I loaned him $200 to help him leave a radio job in Kansas City and move back east. We first met more than a decade ago, when I was a features writer at a newspaper in suburban Philadelphia and he was a freelance photographer for the paper, fresh out of high school. We've remained friends since.

*****

I'm lonely and restless. I want a woman. I want to travel. I want adventure. What shall I do?

I'm already giving thought to taking off for somewhere in a year or two. By the end of this year, Parkway North will be almost too comfortable. This second year is much easier than the first, so far.

As for a woman, no prospects. I don't feel like calling either Cathy. I just don't have that much in common with either. I'm tired of being the one who must take the initiative. Neither one has ever called me.

Charlie has had one woman after another since his divorce earlier this year. He said, "It's easy to find a woman who'll take care of you." Maybe so. But he and I are different. I don't want the same things that he wants.

He, however, is the one with female companionship. I am the one alone.

Monday, September 26

I just went for a long walk. Again what most affected me was passing apartment after apartment, or house after house, in which televisions were blaring away and people were sitting passively. I burn when I see that—burn to be more than I am, burn to be more than just one of millions who let life pass by quietly. But do I burn enough to make something happen?

*****

Charlie was living with his latest girlfriend in his ex-wife's house. She found about his live-in friend and had him evicted. I loaned him $90 so he could move into an apartment. He's supposed to pay me back on Friday. I doubt he will.

*****

Shirley's mother was operated on today. The doctors discovered that malignant cancer is throughout her system. Shirley is up here, but Dave still is in Florida. He called to tell me but barely could talk. He asked me to call Shirley tomorrow night.

He just became the public relations director of the Tampa Bay Bandits in the new United States Football League. Burt Reynolds owns part of the team.

Wednesday, October 5

Robbie called tonight. Talking to him really cheered me up. He's flying in on Monday for a few days of business. He's probably going to talk to my journalism class about his work at CBS.

I came home today really angry. *Norsestar* stories were due today, and a lot of them were poorly done. They are so bad that we won't be able to send them to the typesetter on schedule. Tomorrow I'll begin using harsher guidelines. The honeymoon period is over, I guess.

Norsestar problems simply aggravated my depression. It might have begun on Monday night when I took photos of students decorating the commons for homecoming. A few painted each other as well as posters, and the supervising teacher got really angry at them. I might have made them stop. But I wouldn't have gotten mad at kids for being kids. For some reason, the realization of the difference between that teacher and me made me sad.

Then, on Tuesday, the principal told all about my summer freelance sales at a faculty meeting. I learned later that one of the English teachers told him. To me, those sales, compared to what I want to do, were terribly insignificant, and I was embarrassed.

*****

Norsestar staff placed ads in the *Post* and *Globe*, seeking haunted house stories for our October issue. We've received about a dozen calls. We might spend the night at one of the houses.

Wednesday, October 12

Grace called to wish me happy birthday. So did Sharon. Robbie flew into town Monday and bought me dinner last night. Several students gave me cards and gifts.

The newspaper staff gave me a purple license plate frame with "VIP" on top and "Norsestar Staff" on the bottom. Before class started, girls on the yearbook staff gave me a six-pack of Michelob. I didn't ask how they got it.

As I expressed my thanks and mild surprise, one of them laughed and said, "Well, we heard a rumor that teachers are people too."

Another one quickly added, "Can we open them now?"

"Well, I don't usually start drinking until Freshman English." I smiled. "You'll have to stop by then."

"I told you he would be cool with it," I heard a third say in a stage whisper.

Actually, I wouldn't say I was "cool" with it. But I also knew that it was better that I keep the beer rather than give it back. I wonder if I'm the only teacher ever to take a six-pack of beer home from school.

Some junior girls gave me an obscene coffee mug, complete with jiggling breasts—to drink the beer in, I guess. Mimi, a member of last year's newspaper staff, brought in a cake yesterday. It was good to see her. And it was good to feel loved. I needed that.

*****

Robbie was in town on a media tour for Rubbermaid. I hadn't seen him in four years, and I felt like crying when he left.

He spoke to my journalism class yesterday, along with Don Fandre, a cable TV host and expert on microwave cooking. Fandre is on tour with Robbie.

Following his trip, Robbie will fly to the Seychelles to tour and write articles about the trip.

He is as irrepressible as ever. He went up to four complete strangers, all women, and asked them if they know anyone who would be interested in going out with a "thirty-four-year-old high school journalism teacher." One, a store clerk, got excited and told us about her daughter, Wendy, a twenty-six-year-old who works at Vic Tanny.

Robbie told me about some of his adventures with women. They make Penthouse Letters look tame. That doesn't surprise me. I vividly remember driving his Kansas City radio station's "party van" as he and a young woman attended to business in the back. What I recall most fondly is bouncing across a railroad track, hearing them both scream, and then seeing his panicked face briefly in the rearview mirror.

Robbie stopped back by today. He gave me the business card of a woman who works as a producer at KSDK and told me to call her. Maybe I will.

Tuesday, October 25

I have a terrible infection in the right side of my tongue. I bit it a few days ago. It hurts to talk or eat. Don't know if I'll go to school tomorrow. But I hate to miss.

*****

The last few days have been bleak. More than two hundred Marines were killed by a bomb early Sunday in Lebanon. Today, US forces invaded the Caribbean island of Grenada, following a military coup in which the island's prime minister was killed.

Worst of all, a student of mine got drunk, borrowed a car, and wrecked it, critically injuring two innocent people in the process. She is someone I like very much, and she was someone whom I had great respect for. Now I feel shattered, empty.

Another student told me about what happened because she thought I should know. She was confiding in me, not gossiping. Eventually, though, many in the school will know. One way or the other, word will get out.

I talked to the girl about it. I told her how deeply it hurt me to find out what she had done, but I also emphasized that I still care for her and know how tough the situation is for her. She was afraid, she said, that I wouldn't like her and that what she had done would affect her status on the newspaper staff. I said she still is on the staff and I still like her, but am saddened by what she did.

The car she was driving was destroyed, but she escaped with a few bruises. She said that the parents of the girl who loaned her the car are considering filing charges against her for stealing the car. If either of the people hurt should die, she could be charged with manslaughter.

"I didn't think something like this could ever happen to me," she said.

We sat in the back room for quite a while talking about what happened. She seemed in no hurry to leave, and I was fine with that. I wanted to help her in any way I could. Finally, I hugged her to reassure her that I care, and we left.

Until this afternoon, there had been no sun for eight days.

Sunday, November 6

That infection caused me to miss three days of school. I hated that.

*****

The girl who had the accident told me how much she appreciated my talking with her. Her mother, she said, has had a hard time dealing with the incident. Thankfully, the two people she hit will be all right.

*****

I tried to make plane reservations for a Christmas trip to Florida but was unable to.

Grace said that Linda now plans to marry Ilyker, a Turkish student, as soon as she is divorced from Felix. Oh, yes, that sounds like a great idea!

Linda has so much talent and so much to give. Why does she insist on going from one deep relationship to another?

Grace said she is fearful of being alone. That fear, I'm afraid, never will give her a chance to get to know herself, to find out what she really wants to do and whom she really wants to marry. Doug thinks Linda will let go of Ilyker when she is free of Felix, sort of like giving up a security blanket. I hope he is correct.

Monday, November 21

I've been busy writing articles and short stories, so I've neglected the journal. Dave Precht just told me that he will buy another of my humor essays. This one is "Food for Thought."

*****

Some of my students and I were on local television last night and tonight.

Last night at KMOX-TV studios, we watched *The Day After*, an ABC film about the aftermath of nuclear war. We were taped as we watched, and portions of that tape, including three shots of me, were shown on the late news.

After the movie, we were questioned about the movie, and those interviews were shown on tonight's news. The segment showed a close-up of me as I talked about how the movie made me feel and what I hoped might come of it. I said something like "it was difficult to watch, but if it helped prevent nuclear war, then it was worth it."

Along with the students and me were families, doctors, and a survivalist. I guess we were considered a cross-section. Al Wiman, the station's science and medical editor, asked our school to participate after I asked him to speak to my journalism class on November 29.

The film created a tremendous amount of controversy long before it was shown. I do not think it is a political film. It simply depicts the horror of nuclear war. But it is being used politically by both the "nuclear freeze" and "peace through strength" advocates.

All sorts of warnings were issued about the film, including how it could traumatize the young or extremely sensitive. It was a powerful indictment of war.

But the anticipation was greater than the reality for many, who do not believe the film is as horrible as advertised. Nevertheless, I cried. That's what happens when you're an INFP.

Tonight on TV, the movie was called "the most watched program in history."

In three of my classes, we spent the entire period talking about it. We will write several articles about it for the newspaper. This showing was a historical event, I think. ABC blazed a new trail for television, since the film hardly could be called typical entertainment.

*****

Bonnie Vaughn, my high school English teacher, has asked me to speak to her creative writing classes at Pattonville High School.

Sunday, December 18

Much has been happening, but not enough.

I've rationalized not writing in my journal by the fact that I've been writing so many articles, essays, and stories. My short story, "Frankie's Farewell," has been rejected twice, but with encouraging comments calling it "cute" and "well written" but "not right for us." Dave Precht liked my essay, but bought it hesitantly, he said, because "I'm not sure our readers enjoy fine writing as much as I do."

*****

We just put out the school's biggest newspaper ever, sixteen pages, and finished our first yearbook deadline.

Yearbook work went much easier this time around—except for the work Laura was supposed to do.

She disappeared over Thanksgiving break and did not return. She was on both the newspaper and yearbook staffs. She sent me a letter, telling me about what happened and her plans.

I considered answering it, telling her to stop by and show me her diploma when she gets her GED. I really don't think she ever will. She became one of life's victims at a young age and, I'm afraid, will continue being one, running away, quitting, allowing her life to be determined by those she does not like instead of those she does.

Here's an excerpt from the letter:

"I just didn't think first and now you're paying for my mistakes and I feel terrible. I wish there were something I could do to make it up for it. Even if you never forgive me, I want you to know that you always will be my favorite teacher and I learned a lot from being in your class. No matter how you feel about me, I will always have a tremendous amount of respect for you. And I know what I did was wrong . . .

"I did live it up while I was gone, but I kind of missed school, believe it or not. I lived with my boyfriend for a couple days, then my ex-boyfriend turned me in because I wouldn't marry him. His mom has legal custody of me, but I'm living back at home and I'm going to get my GED.

"Well, that's about all I have to say, except I don't want you to think I wrote this to ease my guilty conscience. You deserve more than an apology, but that's all I can do. I just wanted to let you know that I am not rejoicing over the problems I caused."

But I didn't have to write a reply. I ran into her Friday at Taco Bell. She was startled. I was very careful with my words. I told her to stop by and see me when she gets her GED. She said she will. But I don't have much faith in her to get her act together. The headwinds against her are just too strong.

*****

We just had the AFS auction the same week as newspaper and yearbook deadlines. That's more of what I mean by a lot going on. Summer float trip was bought by seven guys this time. Another English teacher and I also auctioned off a winter float trip. Those two items were the most expensive, as it turned out, bringing in $350 of the nearly $1,600 we raised.

*****

I've been short-tempered at school lately, especially with the journalism class. Part of it has been caused by the students' increasingly lackadaisical attitude as vacation nears, and part of it has been caused by my loneliness, which is more painful around holiday seasons.

One of the teachers has arranged for me to meet a woman over break. I'm looking forward to it. Also, I'm supposed to call a secretary down in Desloge. I met her a couple of weeks ago, where she works for a friend.

*****

I did not particularly enjoy speaking to Bonnie's classes. They weren't very attentive. They made me appreciate my students much more.

Now Mineral Area College in Flat River has asked me to speak at a writers conference on February 14.

*****

Weather is bitterly cold, and my MG Midget won't start. Gas line is frozen, and it's not supposed to get above freezing all week. Someone from Flat River might have to come and pick me up when vacation starts Thursday afternoon.

*****

I've got all my homework done, cleaned the aquariums, watered the plants, practiced juggling, and still am pacing like a caged animal. Not enough to do.

1984

Thursday, January 12

First semester ends tomorrow. I'm glad to be rid of my sixth-hour Freshman English class. In my three years of teaching, it is the most unpleasant class I've had. Four or five created most of the trouble, usually talking when they weren't supposed to. I had to make that class do seat work to keep it quiet, much in contrast to the second-hour class, which has been a pleasure.

My evaluation occurred during second hour. Good marks for my performance. The principal said, "I can tell you are much more at ease than last year."

*****

I've applied for a stipend to attend a six-week seminar on Twain and Swift this summer at Emory University in Atlanta.

*****

My car sat idle for two weeks because of a frozen gas line. Dad had to come and get me for Christmas vacation. Midget finally started on the day that he and Mom brought me back.

For nearly three weeks, the temperature did not get up to freezing. The month was the coldest December on record and the eighth coldest month on record.

*****

I'm dating a third Cathy. Do you see a pattern here?

This one is the sister-in-law of an English teacher at North. She has an eight-year-old daughter by a black man, and she works as an accountant.

The woman whom I was to meet over break did not say two words to me at the party where I met her. The same teacher arranged that, and I wouldn't have gotten to know Cathy if that introduction had worked. I much prefer Cathy.

The rest of Christmas vacation was as uneventful as the party.

Monday, January 23

School is closed today because of icy roads. This is not a good week for a day off. On Thursday, all the yearbook color pages are due. Newspaper stories are due Friday.

Not too many complaints about first-semester grades.

*****

The longer desegregation students are at North, the more problems there seem to be. Last week, two black students beat up a white student in the parking lot. They thought he was someone else, they said. Police and parents were called. The victim refused to press charges. The two received one-day suspensions. One of them live in the district. The other is from the city.

County blacks and city blacks have been involved in several fights with each other. The worst are the girls.

A couple of white girls have told me that the city blacks "bump you around and won't get out of your way" in the halls. Another girl said that they probably do this because they are so outnumbered that they want to show they are tough. I think she's correct.

One black girl, who was in journalism first semester, wrote a story that quoted some blacks as saying they don't want to be at North but are forced to come here by their parents.

Litter and vandalism are big problems this year, but I don't think the city kids are to blame for that. This also is the first year for freshmen at Parkway North.

*****

My poor little Midget, which runs like an old tractor in this cold, is frozen up again. On Friday, I stopped for gas and it wouldn't start after I filled up.

*****

Bad news from *Southern Outdoors*. The editor said he is "not overjoyed" with the photos from my Arkansas trip. Many, he said, are overexposed. He also said that he won't send me on any more trips or buy illustrated features from me until he sees that I have taken some good photos to go with the pieces. He said that he continues to welcome essays and features that don't require art from me. And he added that my Arkansas features are "very well written."

I just sent in another essay. And I have out various other articles, short stories, and essays. I want to write another short story but am having trouble coming up with an idea.

*****

Cathy No. 3 and I have gone out a couple of times and probably will again. Nothing special there, however.

Sunday, February 5

For the first time since my divorce, I've met someone whom I think I could grow to love. Her name is Sarah, and she's a secretary. She's divorced with a seven-year-old son.

We've had two dates and already I feel very close to her. I think she feels the same way.

I live for next weekend, to see her again. It's so wonderful to kiss someone who kisses back, to hold hands, to look into another's eyes and see happiness.

Her birthday is Tuesday. I'm sending her flowers.

*****

Sno-ball softball tournament was this weekend. We went pretty far before being eliminated with a 2–1 loss. Weather yesterday was nice. Today was an Arctic adventure, with temperatures in the teens or below all day, along with winds and blowing snow. It was great!

But I'm afraid I might be getting a cold from the extended exposure. Looks as though that peppermint schnapps between games didn't help as much as I was promised it would.

Mom called to say that she thought she saw me on local news at five thirty. I missed it but will watch at ten. Channel 5 filmed part of one of our games.

*****

I now have a telephone answering machine.

Monday, February 6

I didn't go to school, sorry to say. As much fun as it was to play ball in the cold and snow, I'm now paying the price.

Some more memories of yesterday:

It was so cold my laces froze and I couldn't get my shoes off. Ice crystals formed in my nose.

Vince stood too close to a barrel fire, burned a hole in his pants, singed his socks, and didn't even know it.

Everyone was so bundled up that it was almost impossible to tell the boys from the girls. One umpire said he could tell by the noises they made when someone slipped and fell. A boy went "splat!" A girl went "thud!"

*****

Sharon called about two a.m. one night last week. She sounded frantic and at first wouldn't even tell me what was wrong. She told me to talk to her. So I did. For an hour.

Finally I learned that she had gotten engaged at Christmas and had just broken the engagement, against the wishes of all her relatives. She needed moral support, I think. And I tried to provide it.

At the same time, I remembered what she said last summer, that I don't realize how much she loves me. That weighed on me throughout our conversation.

Sharon said that she just wasn't ready to be engaged. I pray that she is not waiting for me.

III: Heartfelt

Tuesday, February 21

I'm in love. Madly and passionately. More than I ever have been. I grew to love Lois—after I married her because it seemed the thing to do. I love Sarah now and feel as if I always will. With Lois, I never was happy about being married. I wasn't unhappy either really. I simply was.

With Sarah, I'm sure that I wouldn't feel that way. I talk about her eagerly. I show her picture. I want to be with her constantly. Never have I behaved this way or wanted someone so much.

It's wonderful. And horrible. It's torture to be away from her.

Sarah has been divorced since last summer. Her ex-husband was unfaithful to her, and she suffered a lot. She's hesitant to say "I love you" to me. But last night, she said she really wanted to, and she said she had told herself that she wasn't going to "feel this way" about anyone for quite a while. But, she said, now she does.

For the first time, Sarah's son, Danny, is jealous of someone seeing his mother. I'm certain he senses the strong feelings there. But I think that we will get along well.

Still, the fact that Sarah has a child does concern me a bit. A child is a great responsibility, and I'm not sure I can handle it.

But I do love Sarah.

*****

I enjoyed talking about writing at the MAC conference, and the audience seemed responsive. I might be offered a job there. More as it develops.

Sunday, February 27

Sarah said she wants to read what I write about this weekend. I don't know if I can allow that. No one ever has read my journal. It's private.

But then I've never felt about anyone as I feel about her. Maybe she will read this.

We spent the weekend together at her house while Danny was with his father. We had a wonderful time. Well, I did anyway. I can't speak for her. But I think she did.

We spent most of our time in bed. As has happened before with a new lover, my body was shy and I had performance problems. But Sarah was a terrific lover and helped me overcome them.

She finally told me that she loves me. We said "I love you" to each other a lot this weekend.

Both sets of parents know that we spent the weekend together—without us telling them. My sister said that Mom drove by Sarah's at seven a.m. Saturday. I told Mom tonight what we had done: stayed together, that is, not screwed our brains out. And I feel better for that.

After I got back to St. Louis, Sarah told me over the phone that her parents know too and kidded her a little about it. She also said that Bill, her former husband, asked Danny a lot of questions about me.

*****

My sister, Rhonda, and her husband are having severe marital problems. She called me in near hysterics, and Sarah and I went over to see her Saturday night. Joe was out drinking. He does that a lot, it seems.

I urged her to talk to a counselor, and she told me today that she will. I sure hope so.

It appears as if Joe is unhappy with his life as a husband, father, and motel manager and is making my sister miserable as a result. Also, both are playing "gotcha" games simply to hurt the other. I got so sad hearing Rhonda tell about her unhappy marriage. But I'm glad she can talk to me.

Rhonda's story sounded similar to what was going on in Sarah's marriage before it broke up.

*****

Winter float trip was to have been today. But weather forced postponement. We're supposed to get six to twelve inches of snow by tomorrow afternoon. I'm sure glad I made it back up here before the roads became treacherous.

Tuesday, March 7

We had no school for three days last week because of snow. It's supposed to snow again tomorrow.

*****

Sarah had Danny this past weekend, so we didn't have much time alone together.

We played with Danny Saturday afternoon. I fell in the mud, and then the neighbor's giant German shepherd climbed on top of me.

On Sunday, we drove to Elephant Rocks and walked around.

Danny told several lies during the weekend. With one of them, he tried to pit me against Sarah.

He also tested his limits almost constantly. I got really depressed watching one incident. He started by kissing and hugging Sarah, but then wouldn't stop and seemed almost out of control.

At first, I thought maybe I was jealous. But I wasn't. He was being cruel, and that upset me. Sarah and I talked about it. She said Bill used to do the same sort of thing to her.

For the first time, we talked about me playing a role in disciplining Danny. What I'll do, we decided, is offer advice, tell her what I think. It's too early for me to order the kid around. That would cause only more rebellion.

We have enough of that already. It started almost immediately when Sarah and I started dating. We were going to spend the evening watching TV and—after Danny went to bed—cuddling in front of the fireplace. But he refused to go to bed. And when Sarah finally took him by the hand, led him to his room, and tucked him in, he screamed for nearly an hour. It was bizarre, like something out of a movie about a spoiled brat who terrorizes the world.

What Sarah has to do is be firm with him. He feels threatened by me. And he feels threatened by the fact that his father and new wife are going to have a baby.

Sarah said Danny never caused problems before the divorce. But during her year's separation from Bill, she devoted all of her time to him. She even took him to bed with her. I'm certainly not suggesting anything physically perverse happened. But what I suspect is that he now looks at his mother as "his," and I am competition.

Now she has a man in her life and Danny must become accustomed to less attention from her. He doesn't like that, and reining him in is going to be a real challenge. I sure hope it works out.

*****

Rhonda still hasn't talked to a counselor about her problems with Joe.

Monday, March 12

We had more snow today. School closed early.

*****

Jack Lorenz of the Izaak Walton League wrote a letter to *Southern Outdoors*, saying my outdoor ethics article is "terrific." He suggested I enter the piece in the League's ethics writing contest.

*****

The weekend with Sarah went well. As usual, we spent Friday and Saturday getting to know one another better and trying to crowd in as much as possible. On Sunday, we relaxed a bit and truly enjoyed one another in every sense of the word. Sarah said, "I like our Sundays best," and I agree—except for me leaving that night. I don't like that very much.

I had some sexual performance problems again on Friday and Saturday. But Sunday morning, after we returned from church, was terrific. A wrong-number call at the worst possible time Sunday afternoon interrupted us, just before we had to go pick up Danny.

He's still jealous. One way he has of showing it is to ignore me when I ask him questions.

*****

Mineral Area College sent me a job application last week. But I probably won't hear anything before May. Sarah and I haven't yet talked about the possibility of me moving down there. Honestly, I haven't spent too much time thinking about it either.

*****

And speaking of jobs, I've suddenly realized that I haven't written much about this school year at Parkway North. I have different priorities for the journal now, I guess.

*****

Rhonda and Joe had a "long talk." But she still hasn't sought help from a professional.

Tuesday, March 21

First day of spring was cold, wet, and cloudy. We haven't had sun for a week. I sure hope weather is better for spring vacation next week.

*****

Danny threw a terrible tantrum when Sarah put him to bed Friday night. He coughed, gagged, screamed, and cried to get Sarah's attention. Then he told her that she didn't love him. That hurt her deeply, even though she must realize he didn't mean it.

After he said that, I held her and we ignored his cries for about fifteen minutes. Eventually, he came out, apologized, and went back to bed.

Sarah said the tantrum was the worst ever for him. I agree. It wasn't the longest. But it certainly was the most intense and disturbing.

Also, it became painfully obvious during the weekend how Danny tries to manipulate by telling Sarah "I love you." Hearing him at work makes me almost ashamed to tell Sarah the same thing, even though I certainly do love her.

After Friday, Danny was better, but he still has room for improvement.

Part of the problem, I think, is that he has Sarah to himself during the week and then I intrude on weekend. If I were there more often, his behavior might improve. I wish I could be there more often.

*****

No word on the MAC job. Parkway teachers just received a nice raise, which means $2,000 more for me next year. North is a great place to teach in every aspect: good students, involved teachers, and first-class facilities.

*****

NEA Today is going to print my punctuation article in its May issue. That's the same piece I sold to the *Post*. The satirical piece starts with the argument by some language "experts" that punctuation really isn't that important for communication. In agreeing with them, I methodically eliminate punctuation as the article proceeds, until there's none left at the end.

The *Post*, meanwhile, is going to publish my children's self-defense article.

Monday, April 2

Spring break weather was rotten, as usual. But at least I could spend my evenings with Sarah. I love her very much.

I still don't know where our relationship will lead. For me, at least, Danny is the only stumbling block to our eventually getting married. Right now, he lies too much, demands too much attention, and is too disruptive. But I see some improvement and hope there will be more as our three-way relationship develops.

We went to Port Perry on Sunday. Sarah's family has a lot there for camping, near a lake. Sarah and I helped her father and brother clean up the property. Then Sarah and I took Danny and Emily, my niece, fishing.

Emily and Sarah's sister dug worms for us. But Danny refused to get his hands dirty. Then, when I called him up to the car to get his fishing tackle, while struggling to unload the trunk and keep its broken lid open, he said he had to wash his hands. Of course he took his sweet time about it. He constantly must manipulate and control, which is just like his father, Sarah says.

Emily ran up to help me. At almost age nine, she was very well behaved, and I enjoyed having her with us.

On Monday, the neighbor's dog bit Danny in the hand while we were playing. He handled that well. He didn't scream or panic. Sarah said he would have if I hadn't been there.

But he did greatly exaggerate the seriousness of the injury when he talked to his father: "real deep. I'll probably have to have a lot of stitches!"

It was not deep, and stitches were not required.

*****

While fishing by myself one of the few nice days, I saw two men sneak a bass into the truck of their car. They were fishing in Big River, and it's illegal to take bass from the river until the end of May. When a conservation officer stopped by, I reported them. They told him that they caught the bass in a lake and then came to the river. It was their word against mine, the ironclad defense that allows so many people to escape punishment for their misdeeds.

Monday, April 9

Another weekend of rotten weather. But Sarah and I had a wonderful time together.

Our sex life continues to improve, I think, because we love each other so much. Saturday afternoon, we totally exhausted each other and were asleep by ten p.m.

*****

I received my Parkway contract last week, and I have to return it by April 18. I told MAC and North County High School in Desloge that I must know something before then. Yes, I'm thinking more and more that I'll move down there if I'm offered a job.

*****

I'm an uncle for the third time. Jamie Ann was born today. She weighed nine pounds, eight ounces. Everyone predicted a boy but me. Craig and Judy wanted a boy. I guess they'll just have to try again.

Monday, April 23

A couple of my short stories were rejected by publications. *Southern Outdoors* didn't send my ethics article in time for the competition, so I won't be winning any prizes.

*****

I didn't hear from MAC or North County before signing and returning my Parkway contract for next year. The superintendent at North County assures me I will be able to get out of the contract if I want to take another job. He also says he can guarantee me a job for the year after next, if nothing opens up for the '84–'85 school year.

*****

I now have a puppy, a malamute. Or rather Sarah does. She is keeping it for me. I guess she will have it permanently if I don't get a job down there.

We picked up the dog a week ago Saturday when she was only four weeks old. She already was larger than most dogs that are two weeks older. She has adjusted really well and is close to being house-broken.

I named her Cabal. According to legend, that was the name of King Arthur's dog.

According to Sarah, Danny has been really good about caring for the dog. I hope he keeps it up. He certainly needs to learn about responsibility.

*****

Last weekend, with Danny around, everything went all right. But this weekend, when I saw him for only a couple of hours, he acted cold, distracted, and even rude, as he usually does on the weekends he spends with his father. I'm afraid that I'm not feeling any closer to him. He's not very lovable, I'm sorry to say.

On the other hand, Sarah and I are in love, and I see no end to that.

Tuesday, May 1

Danny was at his worst this past weekend. He threw tantrums, he cried, he whined, he lied, and he pretended to be sick. Also, while I was standing in the bathroom doorway, talking to Sarah, who was combing her hair, he squeezed in and tried to slam the door in my face. What a kid.

When we said goodbye Sunday night, Sarah said that weekends with Danny are exhausting. I agree. And they are depressing.

All the way home, I thought about the problem. Then last night I called Sarah and told her that we need to do some things differently. On the weekends that she has Danny, I said, we need to spend one evening away from him so we both can relax. Also, I told her that she must stop letting him separate us when he has a secret to tell her. And I said that I am going to talk to him. She agreed to all three.

I am going to tell Danny that I love his mother, she loves me, and he has two choices: He can be happy with us and have fun with us. Or he can be jealous, misbehave, and get punished. Even if he insists on misbehaving, he will not come between Sarah and me.

I anticipate problems when I tell him that I want to talk to him. Right now, I wouldn't put any kind of behavior past him.

Sarah has tried to talk to him about us. She said that he ignores her or changes the subject.

Part of the problem, I'm sure, is his father's influence. Last weekend, he asked Danny if I spent the night with Sarah when he was there. Danny said I didn't, which is true. Then his father told him that I did when he was not there.

Long ago remarried, Danny's father is a sick, sick man who is interested in Danny only as a tool to hurt Sarah.

Thank goodness Sarah and I have next weekend to ourselves.

Monday, May 7

Still no world from MAC or North County High School.

*****

Without Danny around, Sarah and I had an enjoyable weekend. But again it rained and we couldn't do much outdoors. We did, however, manage to stay busy indoors. As a teacher, I give our sex life an A+. I don't know how much of what we're doing is mutual exploration and how much of it is Sarah subtly leading the way. Before we met, I thought I was experienced. I was wrong.

*****

One of our librarians at Parkway Northway was found dead in his yard this morning. He died sometime yesterday, probably of a heart attack. He was thirty-eight years old and had been at the school since it opened in the early 1970s. Many people were teary-eyed today.

His relatively young age shook up a lot of people, I think, including me. The straw I keep grabbing at is the fact that he was a heavy smoker.

Monday, May 14

The superintendent of North County High School called to offer me a job. But I can't sign a contract until Parkway releases me. The principal here, I think, will pose no problem. He's a good guy. Additionally, Parkway is such a desirable school system that he will have no problem finding a replacement.

Following my release, I will tell the English team leader, and then everyone will know. I anticipate that few will understand, or even try to understand, why I am leaving Parkway, because it's such a great place to work. But for me, there are other considerations.

The thought of moving is a bit depressing. But the thought of living in an apartment any longer is even more so. I'm eager to live in the country close to someone I love and, eventually, with that someone. In the beginning, though, I'll probably stay with my parents for a bit.

*****

Danny posed problems again this weekend. But I refuse to let him come between Sarah and me.

Grace said that the more trouble he causes, the more love he needs. I believe her. But it really is tough to try to love him. He rejects or ignores me every chance he gets.

We spent Sunday at Port Perry. The time with Sarah was great. We fished from her father's boat while her sister watched Danny back on shore.

Tuesday, May 22

Sarah kept Danny until Saturday afternoon because her ex was out of town. We went to a movie Friday night, and Danny went with me to a softball tournament on Saturday while Sarah worked. He was well-behaved both days. For the time, I felt at ease around him because he seemed relaxed around me. I'm guessing the fact that Sarah wasn't there had more than a little to do with his good behavior.

Then he was with his father on Sunday. Sarah said he went to bed crying Sunday night. She said that he told her that her ex told his new wife that he wished he had he never married her. Sarah also said Danny told her about the two of them fighting all weekend and about his father saying he loves—or loved, he wasn't sure which—Sarah.

His father also talked Danny into going with him next weekend by promising to take him to the Lake of the Ozarks.

As Sarah was telling me these things, it occurred to me that the fighting that goes on between her ex and his wife keeps Danny's hopes up that his parents will get back together. That makes it hard for him to like me. I really feel sad and sorry for him.

*****

Parkway North still hasn't found a replacement for me, and I still haven't received a letter saying I will be released when another teacher is found.

*****

Seniors' last day is tomorrow.

Teachers have been very understanding about my wanting to leave. At the same time, they have expressed genuine sadness. I still haven't told students because nothing is definite.

Thursday, June 7, Flat River

School ended last week. It was tough saying goodbye to some of the people at Parkway. But still I'm glad to be moving to the country, where I'll teach the same courses at North County and be closer to Sarah.

And yes, I'm living with my parents. I'll be paying rent on my apartment in the city until August.

*****

Pollen has been terrible lately, and my head has been stopped up all week. I stayed inside all day yesterday and feel better today.

*****

Rhonda and Joe finally have separated. She's staying at the house with Emily.

*****

Sarah and I now see each other every day. It's wonderful. Danny seems better too.

*****

Doug Mayfield, Grace's husband, has an ulcer and a disease that might lead to blindness. They're awaiting test results.

*****

Weekly Reader wants to use my photos of children learning self-defense. They originally appeared in the *Post*. Since my editor at *Southern Outdoors* told me that photos from my Arkansas trip were unacceptable, I've made a concentrated effort to improve. And I think it's paying off.

Tuesday, June 12

My new car was hit Friday night. A truck pushed another car into it. The truck's insurance company is supposed to pay for the repair.

By the way, when I learned I was moving to the country, I traded the MG Midget in for a Ford Bronco, a more appropriate vehicle for life down here, I think. Just call me "Bronco Bob."

*****

Sarah and I took Danny and Emily to Kids' Day Saturday at Busch Wildlife Area. They caught their limits of catfish, and we all had a good time. But Danny is too prissy! Emily helped put worms on her hook. He wouldn't even touch one.

He's spending this coming weekend with his grandparents at Port Perry, so Sarah and I will have a lot of time alone.

*****

My dog, Cabal, already is massive, and continues to grow. I suspect she tops seventy pounds. But with all that hair, it's difficult to tell.

*****

Doug definitely is going blind. But doctor doesn't know how long it will take. He could see for one year, five, or even ten.

*****

Rhonda and Joe are back together. I haven't talked to her in a while.

Tuesday, July 3

Sarah and I had our first major problem.

She thought I was being too mean and gruff last week. And I probably was, mostly because I was tired. I went on a couple of long fishing trips, and we took Danny and Emily to Grant's Farm and the zoo on Friday.

Compounding the problem was the fact that Sarah was tense and nervous last week because she was about to begin a new job.

We walked and talked at Port Perry, and I think we both aired our concerns and worries and became closer as a result.

One of Sarah's main worries is my relationship with Danny. She said that when I try to get close to him, he backs away, and when he tries, I do the same. She also said that he's afraid to get close to me, afraid I'll leave.

I said that I'm trying and it's not easy for me. It's been a long time since I've had a close relationship with one person, I said, and I've never had one with two people before.

*****

Danny has a dachshund puppy. Her name is Heidi. She and Cabal quickly have become playmates, despite the great difference in their size.

*****

Sarah and I are going to the 10th reunion of her high school class this weekend.

*****

The fire department had to rescue my sister's Siamese cat from a tree.

I don't know how she and Joe are doing.

*****

I've been doing a lot of "researching," also known as fishing, for magazine articles, along with writing and photography. And I'll start looking this week for a house to rent or buy.

Tuesday, July 24

I'm helping North County students finish their yearbook, since it seems the previous teacher was a complete incompetent. Only about fifty of two hundred pages had been sent in by the second week in July.

And because I've been so busy with that, I've decided to grit my teeth and stay with my parents until I get settled into my new job.

Wednesday, August 22

I had planned to go to Florida last week to visit the Mayfields and Jovanovics (Dave and Shirley), but I caught the flu and couldn't.

*****

One of my softball friends is a walking accident looking for a place to happen. While target shooting with his bow, he missed the hay bale target and put an arrow through the hull of his neighbor's aluminum boat.

*****

School starts for teachers next week. Kids will arrive on September 4.

Wednesday, September 5

After a Freshman English class today, one of the students told me that she wants to be called "Mrs. Wozniak" instead of her first name, Minetta.

I can't say that I blame her.

Tuesday, November 27

On November 8, Dave Precht called to tell me that he is leaving *Southern Outdoors* to become editor of *Bassmaster*, the company's flagship publication. He asked me to apply for his old job. I did. I'm still waiting for a reply.

I'm almost certain I won't get the job. And the longer I wait, the more certain I become.

As I think about it, that's not a bad thing either. I just left a great job to be near the woman I love. Applying for a job that would require me to move to Montgomery, Alabama, is one thing. Taking it is another.

*****

Sarah's brother told me some "good ol' boy" stories, stuff that maybe I'll be able to use in short stories or novels one day:

—Men who didn't like their boss would get drunk and tear down his mailbox. He finally put up on indestructible one. They tore up a truck trying to tear it down. After all else failed, they took turns pissing on it.

—Several men were in a car that had an overheated radiator. They had no water, and no houses were nearby. They pissed in the radiator. After about a mile, the smell had made most of them sick, and the driver had to keep his head out the window to drive.

—A dog lost one of its hind legs. For two years, it would continue to lift the other leg to pee and then fall over.

*****

Wow. I just noticed a lag of more than two months between journal entries.

Also, most of those used to be about what happened at school. What happened? It's not that I don't like teaching anymore or the students. I do. It's not that interesting things aren't happening in the classroom. They are.

I guess I just have other priorities right now.

IV: Loss

1985

Thursday, January 24

I've been fighting depression a lot lately. Much of it, I think, has to do with the time of year. As best I can remember, January and February are tough months for me.

I sure hope that the season is the main reason. Sarah and I have been having problems too, mostly related to Danny, and I would hate to think that they are so severe we can't work them out and that is why I am depressed. But that's a possibility and likely why I've finally felt compelled to write in my journal again.

I still love her more than I've ever loved anyone, and she says she loves me. But occasionally she's also said, "I wish I didn't." That should be a giant red flag, I guess.

We didn't have any time alone together for a month. I really was down about that and told her so. She said she loves to spend time alone with me but feels guilty about it because she enjoys it so much. I said we have to have that time together to strengthen our relationship.

I don't know if I've convinced her. But I do know I have to have that time with just her. That's why I gave up a great job and moved down here.

She also said that she "doesn't want to feel married," so we haven't been seeing each other as much during the week.

Sarah has had a really tough two weeks at work, with end-of-the-year bookkeeping problems. She's had a lot of headaches and queasy stomachs, and she had cramps last week. Plus, Danny has had the hives on and off for more than a month.

After we hadn't seen each other alone for a month, I broke down and cried, and she said, "I don't think this is going to work."

She wanted to sleep alone last weekend while Danny was away, but we had two really good days together. She seemed more like her old self.

But I know Sarah thinks about her actions a long time before doing them, and I don't know what she's thinking about our relationship.

She talks as if she and Danny will go up to Fenton tomorrow night to see her friend Betty.

Sunday, January 27

I'm so depressed I can't even think or write clearly.

Sarah didn't go see Betty Friday night. She went out with another man. She saw him again last night, the anniversary of our first date.

She told me "it's not what you think." But I know it is.

On Saturday morning, she told me that he asked her out again and that he kissed her. After playing cards with friends last night, I drove by her house about midnight. A truck was in the driveway, and no lights were on in the house.

I told her that I can share her with Danny and give her as much time alone as she needs, but I can't, I won't, share her with another man. I said that I could even do that at the beginning of our relationship, but not now, not after all we've shared.

She wanted to know if I was issuing an ultimatum of some sort. I said that I didn't know what I was doing. I only knew that I hurt more than I've ever hurt before.

I told her that she has to do what's best for her and that I'll back off for a while and not bother her. I told her to call me when she wanted to see me or talk.

She won't call.

The last time I saw her was on Wednesday, January 23.

The pain is almost more than I can bear. I feel hollow inside. My arms and legs seem to be made of lead, and it's hard to take even one step. When I see a small, black car—like hers—I get a lump in my throat.

Mom made biscuits this morning, and seeing them almost made me cry because I remember how much Sarah likes them.

Wednesday, February 13

I spent four hours with a counselor on January 27, and I've seen her four more times since. She's helped a lot. I've finally let go, I think. The following is a letter that I'm sending to Sarah:

"Please don't fear that I will bother you with a weekly letter. This is the last.

"I've endured great pain and anguish during the past three weeks. I still hurt, but I have survived. Numbness now is replacing the pain, and, with that numbness, anger.

"Sarah, I don't care how confused and panicky you became when you suddenly realized we had spent a year together. I don't care how much you 'don't want to feel married.'

"When all is said and done, Sarah, we spent a year together. We were near-constant companions. We shared our most intimate thoughts and feelings. We were friends and lovers in the deepest sense of both words.

"That deep a commitment to one another, whether entered into intentionally or not, carries with it a responsibility. It carries such a responsibility because mutual love and trust have been established.

"That you could be so callous and uncaring to my feelings that you could so easily start seeing another man—for whatever the reason without considering how hurt I might be and without feeling the need to at least explain to me your reasons for doing it—tells me you are, indeed, troubled and confused and that you do need time.

"It also tells me that you were so confused and panicked that any consideration for me was unavoidably forgotten. At least that is what I want to believe.

"I don't want to believe that you did what you did with intention to hurt me.

"I don't want to believe that, but it's difficult. It's especially difficult when, more than two weeks after the fact, you still refuse to provide the clarification I need to ease my suffering and pain. It's especially difficult because not once have you acknowledged my pain and cared enough to say, 'I'm sorry that you are hurting.'

"If at any time in the future you should feel rejected by something I say or do, please realize that my intention is not for it to affect you in that manner, but rather it is to fulfill what I need for myself at the time. I realize now that I can respect another person's needs and feelings, and yet not allow myself to deny my own needs and wants in trying to make that person happy.

"You always will have a special place in my heart."

Thursday, February 14

Here's a Valentine's Day poem I wrote for Sarah:

I wish for you a bed of brass, a car that in cold goes.
I wish for you warm hands and feet and,
  most of all, your nose.
I wish for you some biscuits flat and popcorn by the ton.
I wish for you the best, my love, and also for your son.

Monday, March 11

In a written response, Sarah told me that my letter "really hit hard."

She denied that she was unfeeling and uncaring and insisted that she was sorry that I was hurting. She said that she acted based on what she thought was best for her and Danny.

And she added this:

"I guess you hate me now, as when I pass you, you pretend not to see me. If that's how you handle your needs, so be it. I was just really hoping you wouldn't feel this much hatred for me."

*****

Here's the final letter I wrote to her:

"I don't hate you. If we were to sit down and talk, to clarify, you would realize that.

"I tried my best to get us together to sort things out, to help each other understand what happened and why, and to say goodbye on good terms. You chose not to allow that.

"On January 31, however, you said you 'care a lot' about me and wanted to call several times to talk. On February 7, your birthday, you said you love me. On that same night, after a pleasant one-hour conversation, I asked if we could get together to talk. You said, 'Please, Robert, don't put pressure on me.'

"I haven't. I took you at your word and left to you the responsibility of reestablishing contact when and if you want to.

"I thought long and carefully about what to do for Valentine's Day. I knew you were in a lot of turmoil, and I didn't want to complicate your life by going overboard, sending flowers and declaring my undying love. Instead, I sent you a poem to let you know I care and possibly help you smile a little at shared memories.

"You chose not to acknowledge me on that day, not even by sending a card that says, 'Let's be friends.'

"Not waving at you is but one small way for me to cope with the fact that what we had is over, like returning your key and driving another way so I don't go past your house.

"I won't sign this with 'love' because the word means too much to me. I care too much about myself to go on loving someone who no longer feels the same.

"But I don't hate you. I simply have made the decision to go on with my life without you."

*****

Counseling has helped me deal with this heartache, and I am getting stronger, although I'm not completely there yet. I gave up a life in one place and moved to another for love. I gave up a job I really liked and students I treasured. Now that that is gone, I'm living in my parents' house, and I'm going through the stress yet again of acclimating to a new job.

But I have learned from it, and I will be stronger.

The most important thing I learned is that I can love someone. Honestly, I didn't think I was capable of it, although I didn't know why.

Now I do. Because of my childhood, especially because of a father who abused me, I walled myself off emotionally so that no one could hurt me again. Not even when I was married did I experience what I felt for Sarah. Possibly that's why the marriage didn't work. I was too emotionally distant.

I'm not sure how or why that barrier broke with Sarah. Possibly the guilt I felt for Sharon's unrequited love played a part in it as I recognized her pain and the role I played in causing it. What I do know is that I allowed myself to be vulnerable with Sarah and that I loved truly and deeply for the first time. When all is said and done, that's a good thing.

Counseling has helped me see that. It also has helped me realize that Sarah was, indeed, telling me that our relationship wasn't working for her. She rarely was direct about it, but she was telling me. In looking back at my journal, I can see plenty of entries that provide clues, clues that I was oblivious to at the time I wrote them.

Sunday, August 4

Much has happened since February.

I'm in love with Linda Mayfield, and she says she is in love with me.

But I've decided that I won't move to Miami until next spring. By then, she might feel differently. If she does, however, then I was right not to pack up and move right down there little more than two months after she visited me up here.

On Thursday, May 23, Linda called and said she was coming up for a visit. Her divorce had been final for only a few weeks, and she said that she needed to get away.

I hadn't seen her for three years, and then for only an evening. Before that, I hadn't seen her since 1979, when she was just graduated from high school.

When I met Linda at the airport, my heart nearly exploded. That night, I told her that I felt strongly attracted to her. From there, we became romantically involved, starting in my old bedroom at my parents' house, with them only a few yards away. God, I felt like I was sixteen!

Only I never would have done such a thing when I was sixteen. I was too "good."

Linda said that she would have said something about her feelings for me if I hadn't spoken first.

We had a wonderful few days. We had a picnic at the drive-in movies and then some play time in the back of my Bronco. We watched the sun come up as we lay together on a secluded hillside. We camped at a state park, and made passionate love in a tent during a thunderstorm.

After she flew back to Miami, I went to a writers conference in Phoenix. But my head wasn't into attending seminars because my heart demanded I follow her. So, from there, I flew to Miami as well. Again, our time together was terrific.

Linda again came back up here for a few days. Again, we sought intimacy in the wilderness. No thunder accentuated our lovemaking this time. But we did have watermelon and caviar for dinner.

I spent July with Linda in Miami. We went roller skating in Coconut Grove. We took a road trip to the Keys. We celebrated sunset with the locals at Mallory Square, ate key lime pie, drank Cuba Libres at Sloppy Joe's, and well…made up for what we could not do at her parents' house.

I went with the intent of finding a job and then moving down there. But it was too much too soon after what had happened with Sarah.

I felt pressure of all kinds, especially from Grace, Linda's mother, and balked. I half-heartedly looked for jobs, and, much of the time, I didn't like myself much.

Nevertheless, I was offered a teaching job. That was my breaking point. I called Linda at her job and started sobbing. She came home. I told her that I couldn't move to Miami.

After talking to Grace, I realized that I could, and wanted to, move to Miami, but I didn't want to be rushed. Starting date for the job was August 27, much too soon for me to take the plunge.

I said that I couldn't take the job because of impending deadlines for magazine articles, as well as attending the Bassmaster Classic August11–18. But those were just excuses. I was afraid.

I suggested that maybe I could move down in October.

But even that is too soon. I need time. Only a year ago, I was in love with Sarah. I quit my job in St. Louis and moved to Flat River for her.

Also, although Linda and I have been romantically involved for little more than two months, I have known her for nine years. I know how she focuses on one person or thing for a while and then moves on. I'm afraid of that. I'm afraid that I would move down there and then she would grow tired of me.

Because I'm not going down there right away, I'm afraid she will find someone else to love. I'm afraid of the pressure of a new home, a new job, and a new love. I'm afraid of Grace and her insistence on telling people what to do, although I do love her as my "second mother."

I became sullen and withdrawn while living with the family for the summer in 1978, after helping them move to Miami from Tallahassee. I'm much stronger when I have my own home nearby to escape to, or, even better, when I'm living in another state.

So that is where I am. I love Linda. I want to be with her. But I need time to accept the transition.

By the way, it does make sense for me to move there instead of her coming up here. She's a graduate student in engineering at the University of Miami, and she gets all kinds of financial assistance because Grace works there. Also, Grace and Doug help her provide for Andrew, her two-year-old son.

Wednesday, August 7

A poem for Linda:
I see...
Diamonds in dewdrops,
Laughter in showers,

Promise in rainbows,
Beauty in flowers.

You bring light to my life, my sunshine, and love to my heart.

Thursday, August 29

Next spring is too long to wait for both Linda and Grace, it seems.

In response to Grace's disapproval, I wrote her this letter:

"No, I didn't make a mistake in running toward 'a beautiful, bright woman in a red dress' who clouded my judgment. I love Linda, whether you or Doug or anyone else believes it or not. I never have been confused or questioned my feelings about that. They are real. They are honest.

"Needs are where the trouble arose. I wanted to want to move down there right away. I wanted to make everyone happy. And, at a younger time in my life, I probably would have made the move to please others, denied my own needs, and made the best of things. Linda didn't cloud my contact with myself.

"Until recently, it's always been quite clouded. I did and did and did for others, to get their approval and to be liked, and I wasn't in touch with myself. It's learned behavior. That doesn't excuse it, I know, but that's the way it is.

"My outlook began to change after the breakup with Sarah. With my counselor's help, I saw that I had been set up as the bad person in the relationship because I almost always was the giver, trying to meet her needs and trying to make her happy. She grew to expect more and more from me, and eventually I was unable to give enough.

"With Cindy, the woman I dated briefly before Linda, I had a little trouble at first. But then I saw that she was expecting more from the relationship than I was prepared to give. I had an honest discussion with her about my needs and the fact that I didn't want a deep relationship with her. For the first time, I recognized my needs and acted on them.

"But I didn't have deep feelings for her getting in the way, as they did with Linda. I like Cindy; I love Linda. At that point, I still was all right. I recognized my needs and feelings and acted on them. I told Linda how I felt.

"Then, however, I slipped into learned and accustomed behavior. I loved Linda. I wanted to do everything I could to make her happy, to meet her needs. You were excited. I love you too. I wanted to make you happy.

"Remember one morning in June before I came down there, when Linda, you, and Doug all talked to me on the phone and tried to persuade me to come down there sooner than I had planned? I held firm that time, but I felt extremely guilty about it, as if I were being selfish, even though I had legitimate reasons for staying a few days longer up here.

"Then I arrived in Miami, and the bottom fell out of my self-improvement, recognize-my-own needs plan. Not one time until I turned down the teaching job did I say to myself that I couldn't, or wouldn't, move down there right away. Of course my needs manifested themselves in other ways, especially in my behavior, as I fought to deny them.

"I wanted to want to, for Linda, for you, for Andrew, and even for Doug.

"Yes, I made a mess. I created turmoil. I hurt people. And for all of that, I am deeply, deeply sorry. But finally I acknowledged my needs to some of the most important people in my life, despite the unhappy consequences. I still believe I made the right decision.

"If Linda feels the relationship is over, then I am sorry. I still love her. But I certainly will not fight to sustain something that she does not want. I don't think nine months is too long to wait for two people who love each other. Maybe for her it is.

"In moving down there, I would be the one sacrificing the most, enduring the most change, taking the biggest risk. In waiting awhile, I guess I had hoped to gain some sense of commitment from Linda without making myself totally vulnerable with an abrupt move.

"Grace, I've left four jobs for women. All involved relationships that didn't last, and one occurred all too recently. I didn't realize that pattern until I received the 'Dear Robert' phone call from Linda on August 10. Then, as I was driving and thinking, I suddenly saw what had been happening in my life.

"I really think my psyche realized that in Miami, although I didn't consciously acknowledge it until later.

"Yes, I know Linda is different. Each relationship is different. But we are not robots that act according to what is rationally the right decision or even what is best for us. We are imperfect products of our experiences. Based on my experiences, I need time, time to know Linda loves me, time to come to terms with once more making a move for love.

"I can, and will, get there from here, Grace. I hope that we will continue to be close friends along the way."

*****

So there it is. In my failed relationships with women, I've been emotionally distant to protect myself, while trying my best to please them so they will like me.

Does that epiphany mean my next romantic relationship will be a success? Of course not. But it definitely improves the odds!

1988

Monday, February 8, Flat River

If the world were a kind and compassionate place, we would disagree only about ice cream flavors or movies and we would love equally. Parents wouldn't favor one child over another. And each child would love his mother and father just as passionately as his brothers and sisters did.

Unfortunately, the world is not a kind and compassionate place, and we hurt one another without intending to.

My father died at 12:41 a.m. last Sunday, after more than four months of suffering in Barnes Hospital. My sister grieved and still grieves for him, far more than I, and she cannot understand my lack of caring. Our differences in the love we felt for him and our methods of coping were about to drive us irreparably apart.

Tonight, however, I told her that we needed to talk, and we talked—also yelled and cried—for more than an hour. She does not believe all that I told her, I know. But that's all right if she only will accept the fact it is what I believe and still love me despite our differences. At this point, it seems she will. I hope so. I know that I have problems relating to people sometimes, and I need her love.

*****

For the first two months or more, my mother stayed at the hospital, or with Craig and Judy, hardly ever going home. Rhonda drove up there five and six times a week. I went once a week or once every other week.

I was sick a lot. And I made excuses a lot. I didn't want to go up there any more than I had to.

I have wanted to love my father, and I think that I have tried as best I could. But the feeling never was genuinely there. I feel a lot of guilt about that, and I wish I could be more open and loving toward his memory.

*****

My father was a wonderful material provider for the family. And my mother always said, "He really loves you kids."

But I never felt that love the way that Rhonda, and maybe Craig, must have. I don't remember my father laughing, caring, or sharing. I remember him sitting in his chair at Christmas, not really participating in the opening of gifts. I remember him complaining about his job night after night at the supper table. And, at first, I remember thinking that it sure would be nice when he got a job where he liked the people. But he never did.

He took us on vacations, loaned us money, helped put me through school, and let me live at home at no charge when I moved back here to go to school. He was a hard worker. And, intellectually, I'm sure that he loved me.

But I never felt that he did. And even after I became an adult, I had trouble talking to him.

My sister says she can remember him saying "I love you" to her. I don't. Maybe he did, but I don't remember it. But I think I would remember him telling me what I so desperately wanted him to tell me.

I remember him saying, "Is that all you caught?" when I came home at age sixteen one October evening with the biggest fish that I ever had caught.

I remember him teasing his granddaughters when they were small, saying things like "Are you here again?" when they stopped by with my brother or sister. Of course, he was only "teasing," but sometimes it upset them, and I knew exactly how they felt.

I feared I was unworthy of his love. I tried so hard to please too. I made good grades. I won awards and scholarships. I never got into any sort of trouble.

But never did my father say "Good job" or "I'm proud of you." I tried and tried to win his love, and I always felt I failed.

Perhaps if I had given more to him, said "I love you" before he was lying in critical condition in the hospital, he might have been able to open up to me. But I didn't, and he didn't.

*****

What hurt the most happened when I was eight years old. I didn't realize until eighteen years later the seriousness of the incident, but it had always been in my memory nevertheless. While working for the *Tallahassee Democrat* newspaper, I wrote an article about child abuse and realized that I had been abused.

On Saturday, I had been playing a game with a girl who lived across the street. Suddenly, she leaned across the board and kissed me. I got mad and stormed home.

The next morning at breakfast, my father teased me about what happened. I got upset, jumped up, and accidentally spilled my glass of milk.

He then took his belt and beat me repeatedly on the back, until angry red welts covered it. He was out of control, enraged in a way all out of proportion to my transgression. My mother watched.

A little later, he came into my room, rubbed cream on my back, and said he was sorry. That's the only time I can remember him touching me in a gentle or loving way.

But the damage had been done. I spent much of the rest of my childhood afraid of him. Even as an adult, I never sat near him in their living room.

Years later, when I tried to talk to him about the incident, my father just laughed and acted as if his actions had been appropriate. "You didn't spill any more milk," he said.

*****

My sister refuses to believe I was physically abused. When I told her about it, she laughed in my face and said, "How many times?"

To be abuse, she added, the behavior has to be repeated. It's okay that she believes that, if only she will accept that I believe differently.

While she was visiting the hospital often, she made comments about me at school, where both of us work, because I didn't go to the hospital as often as she. Some people repeated those comments to me, and I mistakenly mentioned that I had been abused, as a way of defending myself. Last week, someone told Rhonda what I had said, and she told mother. That's when I knew that I had to talk to her if we are to stay close to one another.

Our talk brought us closer, I think, and it also revealed that someone I thought was my friend has been lying and exaggerating to my sister about things that I've said. The truth about our differences was bad enough, but he was making it much worse. He's a disturbed person, I fear.

Next, I must have a talk with mother. I told her tonight that I had talked with Rhonda and that we were working out our differences. I also told her that I probably didn't love my father as much as Rhonda and that was part of the problem. She quickly corrected me, telling me that I loved him just as much as Rhonda did, but I just didn't show it in the same way. "You're too much like your father not to have loved him," she said.

Rhonda said Mother told her I was "spanked" for spilling a glass of milk. That's her way of denying the abuse happened and dealing with the fact that she didn't intervene, I guess. What I do know with absolute certainly is that if a teacher had seen my back, I would have been removed from the home for my own protection, and possibly my brother and sister would have been as well.

I don't hate or even dislike my father because of what he did. I know that he must have had a lot of frustration in his life to react the way that he did. And I wish that I could have loved him more. I have been depressed, I think, because I know that I should have loved him more and that I should have grieved more. But I didn't, and all that I feel about my father is a great big emptiness that I wish were love or at least more than I feel.

I did love my father. I do miss him. I just wish that we had been as father and son instead of strangers.

1991

Wednesday, January 30, Flat River

Dave Jovanovic called from Tampa last March and asked to borrow $3,000. He indicated that the loan was short-term and asked me not to tell Shirley, his wife. Knowing how Dave protects her from financial and other problems, I thought that seemed a logical request. He said that he would pay me back $4,000.

Last night, Joyce, a friend of Shirley's who lives in St. Louis, called and left a message, asking me to call her. When I heard the message, I immediately thought that Dave or Shirley might be sick or hurt; Joyce had no other reason to call me.

I called her, and she immediately told me, "Dave and Shirley are dead."

Dead!? My best friends were dead?

An auto accident, I thought.

Then Joyce told me that Dave killed Shirley and took his own life. She knew that he left a note, but she wasn't sure how he killed Shirley.

Joyce asked me if I had loaned money to Dave. She said someone else had too, and he had asked that person not to say anything to Shirley. Joyce thought that gambling might have been a factor.

*****

Bob called this morning. He prints and owns an interest in *Sunshine Classroom*, the bimonthly newspaper for teachers that Dave and Shirley founded after she quit teaching. He said that Dave and Shirley died a week ago Monday. He found them this Monday.

He had gone over on Friday, knocked, hid their newspapers behind the shrubs, and left a note in the door. He went back on Monday, worried because no one knew where they were. The next-door neighbors had a key to the house.

Bob opened the door, saw a note on the sofa, and inhaled a scent that he had learned about in Vietnam. He read the first couple of lines of the handwritten note that was two pages long.

Among other things, the note said that Dave beat Shirley to death with a hammer as she slept. Once he started, Dave said in the note, he couldn't stop because he had to make sure she was dead.

Dave then wrote the note before going out to buy a rifle. Back at the house, he went into the bathroom and shot himself.

"Shirley will go to Heaven to be with her mother," he wrote. "I'll go to Hell."

Bob called that "Catholic school bullshit." He said that I was the only person he told the whole story to.

The note also said, "The lottery is a lie and this will prove it."

Dave had borrowed money from at least a dozen people. Bob estimated he owed $200,000. He seems to have spent all their savings without Shirley knowing it. Joyce said Shirley had at least $65,000 from her mother's estate. Bob said that she spoke of having $80,000 in a credit union in St. Louis.

Bob said Dave hadn't made a house payment since last June. On the day of the killings, their van was repossessed. Dave told Shirley that it had been stolen. That same day, it seems, Dave also received word that they were being evicted.

Back in late December, I had tried repeatedly to call them. Their answering machine, however, never activated so I could leave a message. Finally, I caught them at home. Dave said that there was a short in the phone line, so they couldn't receive calls.

Bob said that Dave disconnected the answering machine and turned off the ringer on the phone because people were starting to call about money they owed.

During that last conversation I had with Dave, we decided that I would visit them in late February instead of late January as I had the previous year. I easily could have been there when he snapped. In hindsight, I have to wonder if Dave orchestrated that change of plans so I wouldn't be there.

*****

Bob said that he knew Dave was in financial trouble because he was owed $15,000 to $20,000. But he had no idea of the magnitude of the problem. Dave was taking every bit of money he could get his hands on and using it to buy lottery tickets.

I never had any idea that he played the lottery. Bob said that it had come up in conversation and Shirley had said pointedly, "Dave doesn't gamble anymore."

Lou, who worked with Shirley, said that Dave occasionally had left them and come back with lottery tickets when the three of them had been on business trips together.

Jeff, another friend, said Dave called him about three a.m. a few months ago and "sounded suicidal." Dave told him that he was about to lose his house, so Jeff gave him $900 and thought that would get him through the tough time. Of course, Dave didn't use the money for a house payment.

Bob said Shirley never knew that Dave was spending all their money, which comes as no surprise. He also said that they dined out three or four times a week, as Dave kept up the charade.

He also often told Bob that one business deal after another was about to come through and he would soon pay Bob what he owed him.

*****

Throughout the seventeen years I knew Dave and Shirley, he always was her protector. She was his little girl, although she was a year older. She was creative and social. He was solid and stable, the person who took care of finances and other worldly problems and sheltered Shirley from care. When she worried—and she worried a lot—he comforted her. He waited on her. He nurtured her. He loved her.

And he killed her.

He must have thought the truth would kill her if he didn't. Or maybe he thought that if he just killed himself, she couldn't survive without him.

So he sent her to Heaven and he went to Hell.

*****

Dave and Shirley were among my oldest friends. In 1973, I first met them in Warrensburg, Missouri, when Lois and I moved there for me to attend graduate school. Shirley often told me that I was Dave's best friend.

D&S and I remained close after my divorce. We went to Key West and Louisiana together. We spend weekends in beach houses. We talked about sports, books, movies, and food. They never allowed me to be depressed. They pulled me out of it by insulting me with absolutely no malice, of course.

I went to the funeral of Shirley's mother and a family reunion of Dave's relatives. I visited them when they lived in Chicago. We ate great Mexican food in a bowling alley, and we went up into Wisconsin to see an artist friend who lived in a train trestle.

They were among the most important people in my life. I thought I was among the most important in theirs. I was flattered when Dave asked to borrow money because I saw that as an opportunity to do something for someone who had been such a good friend to me.

But I wasn't a good enough friend that Dave could reveal his demons to me. He kept them all inside until Monday, January 21, when he could control them no longer and they cajoled him to murder and suicide.

*****

Reaching out to others to help me cope with and make sense of this insanity, I called John and Doug tonight. Doug and Connie loaned Dave $5,000 in September. He asked for $8,000 to $10,000. Doug also said that Schultzy gave Dave the money he had planned to use as a down payment for his own house.

Understandably, Doug was angry, both because of the loan and because Shirley wasn't given a choice.

John said he loaned Dave small sums several times. On the day they both collected their checks from working at the Hall of Fame football game, Dave asked John for $25.

He also said that Dave mentioned going to the horse and dog tracks a couple of times, and Shirley always said, "no," because Dave used to have "a little problem with gambling."

John said that he even had arranged for a friend of his to loan Dave money.

Dave seems to have told everyone the same story: short-term loan, repayment at 25 to 30 percent interest, don't tell Shirley.

I always had thought Dave and I were a lot alike, so I didn't mind giving him the money. I knew that I would rather die than not repay a loan. Dave must have felt that way too.

*****

Friday, March 15

Dave and Shirley aren't dead. I'm at their townhouse in Tampa and they're right there with me.

But they're supposed to be dead, I tell them. I show them a newspaper article that details the gruesome murder/suicide. They laugh and tell me the article was a phony, planted so they could get out from under their debts.

Then I realize part of Dave's head is missing, gore is splattered all over the walls of the house I know so well, a bloody hammer lies on the crimson-soaked sheets, and Shirley...

For the third or maybe fourth time I awaken in a cold sweat from the nightmare.

Over the years, I've had dreams with recurring themes. The two most frequent have been that I'm flying and that I'm lost, unable to get where I need to be. Obviously, the former is a lot more fun than the latter.

Until the death of Dave and Shirley, however, I never had a recurring dream—or nightmare.

Staying busy, I've found, has been the best way to cope. But I have to sleep sometime.

Another vision I can't get out of my head is the double closed-casket funeral in St. Louis, with Dave's family sitting on one side of the aisle and Shirley's on the other. I can't remember talking to anyone, although I'm sure I must have. And I'm not sure how I managed to drive up there and back. But I did.

I'm hoping that a couple of upcoming big events, one of them life-changing, will help me keep my mind focused long enough that I finally can move past this and find a little peace of mind. Of course, I'll never forget what happened. But I need the nightmares to go away.

In late April, I'm going to South Africa on photo safari with a group of outdoor writers. Then in late June, I'm moving to Montgomery, Alabama, B.A.S.S. headquarters, to work full time as an editor/writer. After two years of freelancing, I'm ready to be gainfully employed again.

V: Discovery

Wednesday, May 1, Aloe Ridge Hotel
near Johannesburg, South Africa

On a game drive, we saw Cape buffalos, zebras, waterbucks, eland, impalas, warthogs, and hippos. These were real-life "Hungry, Hungry Hippos" too. Evidently, they're fed on the private preserve where we are staying for one night, and when they saw us they came charging out of the water with mouths agape. I think I managed some impressive photos.

Twelve of us were jammed into a Land Rover that bounced up and down the hilly terrain. The same ride would cost big bucks in an amusement park!

Our driver befriended one of the warthogs eleven years ago when it was young. We fed two of them by hand. They're ugly critters with iron-hard heads and long tusks. They probably think the same thing about us, except for the tusks part.

Oh, yeah, aloe plants grow all over the place.

Tonight we were treated to Zulu dancing and food at a kraal near the hotel. We ate pumpkin, cabbage, maize, beans, and lamb stew. Watching the topless women dancers took me back to my childhood and paging through *National Geographic* for exactly such exposures. I'm guessing some of the other guys experienced the same type of memories.

Thursday, May 2, Kruger National Park

Chuck, the leader of our group, said we saw more buffalos today than he did in the two months the last time he was here. Maybe that's because it's fall down here now and cows still have their spring calves with them.

Sixteen of us, including two guides, packed into microbuses for the trip into the park. Maximum speed in Kruger is fifty kilometers per hour, but we drove closer to twenty-five to thirty, looking for animals.

Once inside the park, visitors are prohibited from getting outside of their vehicles except in designated areas. That made it tough for everyone to get photos of the same animals.

Also, no one is allowed to drive in the park after dark. Visitors must be out or in a rest camp by sunset, which happens quickly this close to the equator.

Chuck said one man got out of his van to take a photo of a lioness. "Before he had taken three steps, the lioness traveled thirty feet and grabbed him," he said.

The man's friends managed to maneuver the van over him to protect him temporarily. But then another lion grabbed his arm and pulled him out. The van went for help.

"All they found of him was his belt buckle," Chuck said.

*****

We didn't see lions today, but we saw lots of other animals, including kudu, marabou storks, ostriches, baboons, giraffes, yellow hornbills, secretary birds, and hartebeest, supposedly the fastest of the African antelopes.

One giraffe suddenly appeared on the horizon in the middle of the road as we motored up a hill. It then crossed the road, stopped, and seemingly posed for us. Nice!

The buffalos liked to look insolently at us with mouths full of grass.

We saw a herd of impalas made up of ewes, young, and one buck. Our guide told us that impalas are the "cannon fodder" of Kruger because of their importance as food for lions, leopards, and cheetahs.

We probably won't see the latter two cats while we're here. The guide said the way to hunt for leopards is to hang a dead impala from a tree.

A leopard can carry twice its weight into a tree, she added. It does so to protect its kill from other animals. It is shy and will not defend its kill from other predators, even from hyenas.

The road was punctuated with elephant dung, but we saw only one animal.

Most of the vegetation we saw was mopani with butterfly leaves and thorn trees, which the elephants eat, along with other greenery.

Sadly, elephants must be culled because they consume so much and use so much water daily. The guide said one will tear down a whole tree to eat only a leaf or two. In earlier times, elephants could range far and wide to eat and drink, but now they must be more restricted if they are to be protected—and agricultural land is to be protected from them. One elephant can destroy a thousand hectares of sugarcane overnight.

Kruger can accommodate seventy-five hundred elephants while annual culling eliminates their need to migrate. They are culled in family groups. Managers discovered that was more "humane," the guide said, because of the heart-wrenching way survivors mourned if only one or two in a group were killed.

Profits from products made from their hide and hair go to help manage and protect the remaining population.

Poaching still is a problem, especially by those who want ivory. Fences have been put up along the eastern border with Mozambique to keep the elephants in the park and the poachers out.

By the way, Kruger is about the size of Israel and generally considered the best animal park in the world, according to the guide. It is home to one hundred and thirty-three species of mammals.

Friday, May 3

Baboons woke me up twice last night. They sound a bit like dogs barking and babies crying.

Animal facts and lore from our guides:

Cheetahs are sloppy eaters, while leopards are more meticulous. Cheetahs get their speed from super doses of adrenaline.

Female giraffes have fuzz on their horns. Males do not. Males get darker as they age.

Hippos kill more people than any other African animal. A hippo can "eat about a ton" of vegetation daily. (That seems an extraordinary amount to me.) It then defecates along the shoreline and "splatters it all over." Legend says hippos splatter as a way of telling the lion, the king of the jungle, that they are not eating fish, which was the lion's condition for allowing them to live in the water.

Right away this morning, I spotted an elephant just to the left of the van. The man on the passenger side dropped a lens as he hurried to take a photo and then, without thinking, opened to door to pick it up.

The elephant trumpeted, flared its ears in alarm, and walked away. But then it turned and moved into the road in front of us. It trumpeted again and looked as if it were about to charge. The guide whipped the van into reverse, and we beat a hasty retreat. He said five vehicles in Kruger have been attacked by elephants.

A little farther on, we saw a herd of waterbucks on a hillside. The morning sun glistened on their horns, and they all stared out toward us in the warm glow. The scene had an almost religious quality.

*****

Chuck told me that a magazine article stated that the Afrikaans white male is the largest male of any nationality. That helps explain why so many of the urinals I've seen are over waist high for me!

Saturday, May 4

Downriver from where we saw a large concentration of hippos, as well as crocodiles, we stopped to look at elephants on the shore to our left. Suddenly to the right, a big one came strolling down the path toward us. When it saw us, it raised its trunk and stopped.

I had been taking photos of the river elephants from the top of the vehicle, and two others joined me. When the angry elephant started toward us again, swaying and swinging its trunk, the guide told us to get in the car.

Being the gentleman that I am, I allowed the other two to get down first, as I continued to take photos of the pissed-off elephant coming our way.

I then tossed my camera down to Chuck and jumped from the top, landing butt-first in a pile of elephant dung. Fortunately, it was mostly dry. Even if my photos aren't good, the "essence" of that adventure will linger with me.

During an afternoon drive, I was sitting near the left sliding door of the van when an elephant decided to cross the road from left to right just in front of us. It blew dust with its trunk as it paused and looked at us. The woman behind me yelled, "Close the door! Close the door!"

No way! I think I got some great photos.

I also managed some nice close-ups of vervet monkeys. One looked as if he was playing an invisible guitar as he raised one arm to scratch under his other.

*****

The guide showed us a large tree with a light yellow trunk. He said it was called a "fever tree" because people used to think it caused malaria. Actually, it only grows in malaria areas, so it's guilty by association.

*****

We've yet to see lions, but today we saw tracks. If we don't seem them tomorrow on the way to Skukuza, we almost certainly will at Ngala.

Sunday, May 5

Most of today was a waste of time because of vehicle problems.

This area of the park is supposed to be the best for lions and rhinos, but we don't get to find out. Tomorrow we must leave early to go north, the direction we came from today. If we had stayed at Olifants, we would have had a quick drive to Ngala, a private preserve noted for its big cats. So we hurried down here for nothing, and now we have to hurry back.

Oh, well, shit happens.

At least at Ngala we will go out in open vehicles and we don't have to be in camp by five thirty p.m. The staff also should have a good idea where the big cats are.

*****

For dinner we had kudu filets and buffalo kabobs, among other delicacies, as well as good South African red wine.

During our meal, a park official told us that Africa has 600,000 elephants and the population is "nowhere near being extinct." He also said that private landowners are making more money with wildlife than cattle, and land on private preserves has more animals than it did a hundred and fifty years ago.

Monday, May 6, Ngala Private Game Reserve

We had a great experience this evening. We were surrounded by lions. Some of them got within ten feet of us.

One seemed curious, but the rest just yawned or stopped and scratched themselves as they strolled by. Some of the young ones jumped playfully at one another. The pride consisted of two adult females and eight that the guide estimated were eight or nine months old.

They appeared just at dark as we were sitting by a waterhole in the Land Rover, looking for wildlife on the other side of the water. I hope I managed some good photos, but, even if I didn't, the experience was superb.

During the minutes the lions were around us, all my senses seemed extra sharp, which heightened the experience. I could smell the cats and the water where they had been drinking. I could feel the chill in the night air. I could see the lions' eyelashes and whiskers through my camera lens.

The guide whispered that lions and other animals are not afraid of the Land Rover or the spotlight, as long as we don't stand up and show them humans are present. He added that fumes from the exhaust mask our odor.

*****

Before the lions, I took good photos of a crocodile, white rhino, and kudu. We walked to within fifteen feet of the twelve-foot croc, which opened its mouth but stayed put. Only afterward did I notice that the guide did not join those of us foolhardy enough to get so close to the croc.

We also saw two leopards and a cub, but could get no photos.

We stayed out until about eight thirty. A few of us are going back out at five in the morning before we all fly to Cape Town.

I'm writing this by lantern light. The generator shut off at ten.

*****

This was the first night we had been out of camp after dark. Never have I seen so many stars. I just kept staring up as we waited for the cats. One falling star lasted at least five seconds in the crisp, clear night.

Many of the locals seem acquainted with the constellations, meaning, I guess, that the sky is special for them too.

*****

As we were bouncing down a dirt path, a huge insect (I think) ricocheted off me and Terry, who was sitting beside me. It then fell in my camera bag before coming to its senses and fleeing. It was too dark to see what it was. But during daylight, we have seen grasshoppers and katydids of Jurassic proportions.

Tuesday, May 7, Lambert's Bay

I didn't get much sleep. Chuck and the baboons kept me awake. In Kruger, the drone of the air conditioner drowned out Chuck's snoring. But at Ngala, the generator shut off at ten.

But I'm having such a good time, I don't mind a little sleep deprivation, especially since that keeps me from having nightmares about Dave and Shirley. Actually, I'm not dreaming about them much when I do sleep either. My mind is too filled with thoughts of what we saw each day and what me might see the next. This mind rinse is a very good thing.

*****

We got some great shots of lions (I hope!) early this morning. Lee, our guide, drove right up near them with the Land Rover, and one of the big cats finally lay down to pose for photos. Lee said the two were about two and a half years old and probably had just been run out of the pride they grew up in. Now they have to find their own.

Until a lion is a year old, it has only a 50 percent chance of survival because of possible predation by other lions, leopards, and cheetahs, Lee said.

As predators, lions are 50 percent effective in getting their kills. Cheetahs and leopards are 50 to 70 percent, while wild dogs are the most lethal at more than 70 percent.

We also saw hyenas, jackals, and a honey badger (relative of our wolverine), as well as vervets and baboons.

*****

I asked Lee about the sport fishing. He catches yellowfish, barbells, and tigerfish, as well as bass.

In Africa, he said, a fisherman can't relax too much or he will become the prey. Hippos are especially dangerous. They often attack boats passing through their territories.

*****

After our early-morning game drive, we spent about fifteen hours traveling cross-country by plane and car to the West Coast. When we checked into the Marine Hotel about eight p.m., the area was blanketed in fog and probably will be tomorrow morning as well. We're supposed to visit a bird preserve—lions today, penguins tomorrow.

This part of South Africa looks totally different than Transvaal area. Cape Province has broad, flat fields for sheep and crops, encircled by mountains. It's the end of the dry season, so most fields are brown and we saw lots of dust in the air. We also saw two large fires during our three-and-a-half-hour drive from Cape Town.

I finally got to see famous Table Mountain at Cape Town. It's mentioned in most of the Wilbur Smith novels I've read.

Cape Town is a scenic city on a rugged coast and particularly beautiful now with jacaranda blooming.

Near the top of one mountain, we stopped to look at the land below us and take photos as the setting sun peeked between peaks. Clouds diffused the light and turned the sky red and orange for a gorgeous sunset.

Wednesday, May 8

I hardly slept again because of Chuck's snoring. Don't know how much longer I can endure this. To put some distance—and a door—between us, I finally moved to the bathtub about two a.m.

The morning was cloudy and foggy, but light was good for photography at the conservation island across the road. I managed lots of shots of gannets and endangered jackass penguins.

The gannets numbered in the thousands. Packed together, they fussed and preened, and pairs raised their long necks together and almost intertwined them.

I saw only one penguin for a long time but then found their nests among the rocks. Their nearly grown young are two to a nest. As I sat, waiting for them to climb out into the open, some of the young ones brayed, making it easy to see where they got their name.

During a short drive to a "salt pan," we saw flamingos, sacred ibis, oyster catchers, herons, and other assorted birds.

*****

We had lunch at a place on the beach called "Muis Bos Kerm" (Mouse Bush Enclosure). It's an open-air restaurant enclosed by a kraal of brush. Bread was baked in a clay oven, and other foods were grilled or boiled over open flames.

We had snoek (relative of barracuda), mullet, and brim—all grilled—as well as fish stew and a wonderful South African version of paella that featured rice, onions, mussels, crayfish (rock lobster), and fish. We also enjoyed corn, potatoes, hot bread, dried pilchards (fish jerky), watermelon, good South African white wine, and coffee.

Price was 40 rand, about $16, for best meal so far.

Oops! Almost forgot the main course —grilled rock lobster that we ate with our hands. We used mussel shells as spoons for the stew and paella.

*****

Not surprisingly, considering the name of the place, mice live in the kraal and can be coaxed out for tidbits.

The area is barren and rocky in many places, resembling Cape Cod. A few sheep graze the fields, and potatoes are grown as well. Beaches are white and water is emerald, with a touch of blue.

While "blacks" make up most of the population of the Transvaal, this part of Cape Province seems to have a lot of "coloreds." They are descendants of early Dutch and native Bushmen, as well as Dutch and Hottentots. Their skin is a burnt gold color. Some have sharp features and others have broad noses. In general, they seem a smaller people.

As with blacks in the Transvaal, they provide the labor force. Often our luggage is carried by the maids, some whom balance it on their heads as they transport it to our rooms. Tomorrow we head back to Cape Town for a tour of the coast and dinner with the mayor.

Thursday, May 9, Cape Town

I'm dead on my feet from lack of sleep. I don't know what I'll do tonight. Maybe I'll move my mattress into the bathroom, if it will fit. Bathtub isn't very comfortable.

*****

Today we drove down the coast and on to the Cape of Good Hope, the southwesternmost point on the continent of Africa. I took lots of seascape photos.

Enroute, land mostly was bleak and barren, but then greenery popped up, including orange groves and vineyards.

The Cape itself has few trees, but lots of low-lying vegetation and rocks everywhere. Our guide called the shrubs and wildflowers "fynbos." Some said the land looks like Scotland. I thought it looked a bit like the mountainous shore on the island of Kauai in Hawaii.

Our guide said South Africa has about twenty thousand species of plants, with seventeen hundred at Cape Point, the seven-thousand-hectare reserve on the Cape.

On the way to the Cape of Good Hope, we passed False Bay, so named because the Portuguese thought it was the shortest route they could follow around the end of the continent. Vasco da Gama named the Cape of Good Hope on his way back from Dutch East Indies in 1498.

After dinner with the mayor tonight, we'll go to Upington and Augrabies tomorrow.

Friday, May 10

Wind was too strong for a cable car ride to the top of Table Mountain. But we got some good scenic shots of Devil's Peak, Table Mountain, and Lion's Head. Then we had about three hours of wandering around Cape Town, where we actually saw Archbishop Desmond Tutu crossing the street.

In the afternoon, we enjoyed wine tasting at Constantia, the oldest winery in South Africa. I liked a "floral sauvignon" the least and a port the best. I would have ordered a case of the latter if it could be shipped to the US. But trade sanctions remain in place as the country slowly dismantles apartheid.

*****

I finally got some sleep last night. A sleeping tablet helped.

Before that, dinner with the mayor went well. Chuck and I sat with him and the "mayoress." The mayor said Cape Town has been "mixing the races" for several years and praised his city as being more liberal than most.

The mayor is a slender man with a beard who reminded me of a Quaker farmer. He's a vegetarian.

As we walked the streets, we often were asked for money by "colored" women and children. The women usually asked for money to buy food for their children.

Wind blew hard all day, with some streets acting as wind tunnels and others dead calm. We were told that property buyers must be careful because of the way winds blow between and around the mountains. Some areas are far windier than others.

Cape Town is a beautiful town with red tile roofs, white sand beaches edged by rugged rocks, and a Mediterranean climate.

Saturday, May 11, Augrabies

Augrabies Falls National Park is like Elephant Rocks State Park in Missouri magnified a million times. Granite cliffs extend for miles along the Orange River, and huge boulders are scattered about on the flat tops of those cliffs.

Several waterfalls pour down the rocks all along the river. In one place, I saw three separate branches of the river, each with its own waterfall. It's spectacular to see because the land is so rugged and the water so fierce. But there's little to photograph—red and brown rocks with muddy water.

On the other hand, wildlife has been an unexpected bonus. I've taken lots of photos of klipspringers (antelope), dassies, and the Cape flat rock lizard. The latter is turquoise in front and orange in back, with yellow legs.

Dassies are small, rodent-like creatures related to—believe it or not—elephants. "They urinate and defecate at fixed spots," a brochure says. And I can vouch for that. Droppings blanket the ground in places, and the stench of pee is almost overpowering.

I first saw them when I stepped into a depression between boulders. I saw one, then another, and another, and another. With all of them watching me, I felt like a cowboy suddenly surrounded by Indians.

Then I spied a female klipspringer munching leaves on top of a bluff. I snapped a couple of quick shots with my telephoto lens and then started sneaking forward. I put down my camera bag so I could move more quietly and quickly.

I kept snapping photos and inching forward until I was about twenty feet away and she was so close I couldn't fit her in the viewfinder of my camera.

That's when I saw the male, with his short spiked horns, and heard the distressed bleat of a young one. I quickly shot the male and then found the lamb. I probably spent a half hour perched on a cliff, watching the three and burning more film.

The female was nonchalant, even lying down at one point. The male was on guard, constantly sniffing the air. The lamb stayed in one place and bleated.

Then came the big scare. I had a devil of a time finding my camera bag. The terrain is so broad and so similar that backtracking was almost impossible. But I did it.

In the afternoon, our guide pointed out aloe "quiver" trees. He said Bushmen hollow the branches to make quivers for their arrows.

Fuzzy white grasses on the vast red landscape were beautiful in the evening sun.

*****

For lunch I had the South African version of lasagna, or so the menu said. But it contained no pasta. Instead it consisted of meat and mushrooms covered with whipped potatoes and cheese. Restaurant also offered "snail kabobs." I wasn't feeling that adventurous.

Breads and fruits in South Africa have been great. Meats are pretty tasteless and/or tough. Breakfast bacon invariably is rare and dripping grease.

We are going on a game drive three thirty a.m. tomorrow. But today will be tough to beat.

With the help of another tablet, I got some sleep again last night. What a difference rest makes!

Sunday, May 12, Gemsbok National Park

I didn't enjoy today and am feeling frustrated by my inability to do anything about it.

First, the ride up here to Gemsbok National Park in the Kalahari Desert took five hours.

Then, staff did not have lunch prepared for us as they were supposed to. Also, they tried to put us four to a room, instead of two, and there was much haggling about that.

But, yeah, I realize that I'm travel weary and that probably accounts for most of why I'm feeling whiny.

Finally, about three p.m., we went out for game viewing, having to return by six. During those few hours, we did see a female lion wearing a radio collar. We also saw bat-eared foxes, springboks, gemsboks, ostriches, wildebeest, goshawks, secretary birds, meerkats, and a tawny eagle. But we didn't see great numbers of animals, as Chuck said we might.

I suggested some of us skip breakfast tomorrow (seven thirty to eight thirty) and go out at seven when the gates open. Our guide didn't seem to like that idea, although he didn't say so. Everyone else did.

The pace is much slower in this part of the country, especially in restaurants. For example, we had a one-course dinner that took an hour.

Also, most everyone underestimates how much time things take. Our guides invariably tell us trips take less time than they really do.

Another maddening thing was a slideshow that the staff insisted on presenting to us before we went out this afternoon. We were told it would take ten minutes. It took thirty. We also were told the ranger drove a hundred and fifty kilometers or so to present it to us. I said that we drove nine thousand miles to take photos, not sit around.

*****

Kalahari-Gemsbok is about 960,000 hectares in South Africa and a million in Botswana. With an adjoining preserve added, the total is 3.2 million hectares, making this the largest game preserve in the world.

This remains one of the wildest areas in South Africa. Animals here still can migrate, contrary to Kruger and other places where they are enclosed.

Animals here depend on cucumbers and melons for water. Rainfall here averages less than two inches annually. For nine years out of ten, these fruits—yes, cucumber is a fruit—can keep animals alive if no rain falls. But if the plants die, they must migrate. If fences stop them, as they do in some areas of this vast wilderness, then the animals die along the fences.

Much of the park is semi-arid savanna with camelthorn trees (acacias). Dunes are to the southeast, with flatter land to the northeast and forest to the northwest.

The Kalahari is named for the Bushman tribe that settled the area eight hundred to nine hundred years ago. And that reminds me: "Augrabies" is the Hottentot word for "place of great noise," which is appropriate because of the many waterfalls.

*****

During the drive here, our guide told us about a manhood ritual for Zulu and Xhosa boys. As teens, they're circumcised and then clothed in tall straw hats and grass skirts. Their faces are covered with white clay. They remain that way, usually isolated, for several weeks.

He also said that Zulus and Xhosa still won't recognize men in positions of authority if they haven't gone through the ritual. He said Zulus won't work for Xhosa bosses, and Zulus never would consent to being governed by a Xhosa.

Nelson Mandela is a Xhosa.

*****

Also on the drive, we stopped at a South African police station to use the facilities. Across the dirt road, we saw some black children in their Sunday finest, returning from church. They were eager for us to take their photos, and we obliged. One little girl in a peach-colored dress delighted in making faces.

Monday, May 13, Upington

We went out about seven fifteen, and viewing was slow until we spotted springboks and gemsboks along a hill, with a path leading among them. We followed the path to the top and took some great close-ups of the gemsboks' beautiful black-and-white faces.

Suddenly, our guide whispered, "Cheetah!"

We turned to where he was pointing and saw one of the big cats appear regally on the horizon. Another followed. And a third. We were so excited we could barely contain ourselves, as we snapped photo after photo.

As we had noted before, the cats didn't seem to mind our presence as long as we remained in the car. One did pause and look our way, making for a memorable moment, as his spotted coat glistened and the sun reflected off his black eyes.

Then the three loped down the hill toward the antelope, which fled. But the cheetahs paid them little attention. Two of them lay near a tree, and the other kept watch. We hoped we might get to see a kill.

But then I spotted the remains of a springbok, and we realized they already had breakfast.

We also saw rooibok and steenbok, as well as secretary birds, black wildebeest, black-backed jackals, and assorted eagles. We didn't see nearly as many meerkats as I hoped we would.

*****

The drive to Upington was awful, mostly on a rutted dirt road. Our guide refused to put up his window, even though we asked him to four times. Our hair, clothes, and luggage was coated in dirt by the end of the five-hour ride.

Some of the guys think he did it intentionally because we didn't want him to smoke on the morning game drive. That was because one of them had been a heavy smoker and had to have heart surgery.

During a rest stop, I took photos of locals in a horse-drawn wagon.

*****

Despite occasional complaining, I've had a great time and a great adventure. Tomorrow we return to Johannesburg. Everyone but me will fly home. I'm staying to do some fishing with South Africa B.A.S.S. members.

Chuck, our group leader, said he heard on the news that Winnie Mandela has been found guilty of all charges for kidnapping and accessory to assault.

Friday, May 17, Heyshope Dam

Local anglers have been very gracious hosts. We caught bass in the Vaal River, which is lined with tall grasses and huge willows. I saw blue monkeys, deer, and lots of birds. Carp fishermen frequent the river, using log rods and motorized toy boats to take their baits far out from shore.

*****

On our way here tonight we stopped in Ermelo for gas and to see a friend of Shawn and Kevin's. He's an Indian Muslim named Josef, who owns a market and a transport business. They met through bass fishing.

Josef insisted we go to his home for a meal. He lives in the Indian section of a black township.

His family is preparing for the wedding of his daughter on Sunday. We were seated in an outside room covered with canvas, where a dinner for fifty or sixty will be Saturday. About five hundred will attend the wedding.

We had authentic Indian food—several curries and a flat pita-type bread. Curries contained liver, spinach, chicken, and potatoes. Everything was made from scratch and seasoned with home-grown ingredients. It was delicious!

We ate with men at one table. Women ate quietly at another. Most women were dressed in traditional gowns and veils, but a few girls were not. Most of the men wore various types of skull caps, with one in a balaklava.

Shawn and Kevin ate with forks. I joined the Indians and ate only with my right hand. I enjoyed watching the men eat and lick their fingers.

It was funny to see Coca-Cola bottles scattered in this setting with traditional Indian food.

As we ate outside in the cool night air, Josef said, "We used to shit outside and eat inside. Now we shit inside and eat outside. This is progress?"

Saturday, May 18

We fished for about five hours and got one bite. Cold temperatures, not much above freezing, didn't help. I had no idea it could get this frigid in South Africa. I'm really grateful for the loan of a coat, gloves, and sock cap.

About eleven thirty, we talked with Tim Williams from Natal. On his second cast with a crankbait, he caught a four-pound-plus bass.

Heyshope is surrounded by flats, except for hills and rocks at one end. With wind, the water can get rough really quickly. Elevation is about forty-five hundred feet, and mountains are in the background.

We saw goats on the steep end of the reservoir, as well as lots of coots, yellowbill ducks, teals, Egyptian geese, and cormorants. Kevin said many more are here in summer when the aquatic grasses are growing.

We found a dead cormorant with a one-pound bass in its mouth and throat. The fish didn't die alone.

We also watched a family of otters at play. One youngster was curious and stayed near as we approached. Finally, the mother pulled him away.

Sunday, May 19

We fished until noon, and still no bass. In fact, we didn't see fish of any kind. Tim caught one more early and then had no bites either.

On the way back to J-burg, Shawn and Kevin drank heavily. Castle beer was the alcohol of choice.

Monday, May 20, Durban

A local named Kevin is one of those who will take me bass fishing at Albert Falls. He's also the most interesting character I've met in South Africa.

As with other whites I've met, he moved down from Zimbabwe soon after blacks took government control. Ken refuses to call the country anything but "Rhodesia" and still carries the fear of black/white violence with him.

He was in the Rhodesian army for twenty-six years, and he has killed people. He also is an ardent fisherman, and, while war was going on, he continued to fish the Zambezi River and other waters of his homeland.

He also raised adders for their venom. Ken said snakes become docile faster around humans than any other wild animals. "Four days is about all that's needed," he explained.

Tuesday, May 21

I had a very enjoyable day. We slept in and didn't go fishing at Albert Falls until about ten a.m. About a half hour later, Eric caught a two-pound-plus bass on a twitch bait. I hopped over into Ken's boat and took photos of him "re-catching" it. As I've become a more experienced outdoor writer/photographer, one of my most important discoveries is that most fishing photos are staged.

At noon, something big hit my twitch bait. It actually pulled line off against the drag. I was afraid it was a large barbel (catfish) since we saw lots of them around us. Eric told me later that he thought so too but was afraid to say anything.

Then a big bass exploded on top and we both got excited. I put the rod tip low to keep her from jumping. Once more she pulled out line, and several other times she nearly did. Finally, Eric slid the net under her.

She weighed 2.3 kilograms, or five-pound-plus, and was the hardest fighting bass for her size that I've ever caught. Eric said that was because she's "Natalian."

Ken was a good sport and posed with my fish for photos. He also took some of me with my camera.

Wednesday, May 22

Today was a tourist day. Early this morning, Eric and I drove up into the Drakensberg Mountains, northwest of Durban. On the way, we passed through Zulu lands, where women carried bundles on their heads, and little boys herded cattle along the road.

In the Drakensbergs, we hiked up to caves where Bushmen had lived and painted hunting scenes on the walls. Bantu tribe and whites eventually drove Bushmen out of Natal in the 1870s. At first, they were hunters only, but, when others moved in with cattle, they became thieves.

On our way out, we saw a herd of eland, the largest antelope. And they are massive, especially compared to the little klipspringers I saw in Augrabies.

Drakensbergs rise to about fifty-five hundred feet. Zulus call them "pile of spears." They are sparsely beautiful and remind me of Western Nebraska.

Trees in the mountains are deciduous and showing their red and yellow fall colors. It's difficult to believe this is Africa. But Zulus are constant reminders, as are the thatched huts they live in.

*****

We had lunch at the log cabin home of Eric's friends. They live not far from the Bushmen paintings. They have a trout pond in front, and Mike is building a bar near it so he and his mates can sit outside with drinks and watch the trout rise.

Mike also raises hybrid guinea fowl for market. He said leopards, servals, and lynxes are a big problem during winter. They dig under the wire and get the birds or simply scare them to death with their presence.

Three Zulu herd boys found leopard cubs last year and decided to keep one of them, Mike told us. The mother leopard killed two of them and the third escaped only by sliding down a mountain. A search party discovered the bodies nearly decapitated.

Mike also said he nearly was eaten by a lion during a drive through a private game preserve. The lion climbed onto the bonnet (hood) and tried to break the windscreen (windshield) but couldn't get through.

His wife said she can't keep roses because the antelope eat them.

Thursday, May 23

I'm sitting at the beach, enjoying a little time to myself. Out in the dark blue ocean, under a light blue sky, a large cargo ship is passing. Nearer shore, a kayaker paddles by and a parasailer is descending. A surf fisherman has his lines out near an old pier, and some sun worshipers with golden tans and yellow hair are bringing in their rubber raft.

Behind me, pigeons crowd a promenade, awaiting handouts, and African women stand in the sun, with their crafts for sale.

An hour or so ago, Ken talked to me again about race in Africa. He's an intelligent, rational, and pragmatic man. And he's afraid that South Africa soon will go down the same path as other African countries. Here is what he told me:

"Now, we (whites) are down here, they (blacks) are up there (Zimbabwe) and no one is better off. What was it (overthrow of white rule) all about?

"I tell people to show me one, just one, example where Africans have built a bridge, developed a community, or done anything creative. They don't build, invent, or create. They take, use up, and destroy.

"I can show you dozens of cases where they've taken over and destroyed everything. Stupid countries like America and England keep sending them aid. If they didn't, they (black-ruled countries) all would be dead.

"We've allowed them to reach the point where they want to take over. We've allow their populations to grow until they're a majority. They didn't used to be.

"They killed malformed babies. They died of disease and in battle. They were ruthless with each other. Then we came in and said, 'No, no, you can't do that. You must be civilized.' So now there's many more than there were before because of us.

"Every African tribe believes it's better than another, and it always will be that way. Africans are the most intolerant of other races. Just look at what happens when they take over.

"Yes, I am a racialist, but I don't care who rules if the leadership is good quality. Africans haven't shown me they can be that way.

"Look, if a lion bites you, you're going to avoid getting too close to other lions. You learned.

"And the argument for majority rule doesn't make sense. Do ants rule the jungle because there are more of them than lions?

"Whoever rules is going to be hated by some. That's the way things work.

"I'm afraid things are really going to deteriorate here."

Ken keeps a pistol in a small gym bag and takes it with him everywhere he goes.

*****

I didn't ask Ken to talk to me about race, and I'm not sure how I feel about what he said. But it does make an interesting addition to what Lazarus, a black taxi driver, told me a few days earlier. Lazarus is a Sotho and speaks Sotho, Zulu, Afrikaans, and English.

I did ask him about the race issue because a recent newspaper headline screamed "City's 24 Hours of Terror" following bombings in Johannesburg.

"South Africa is a beautiful country," he said. "But they always are fighting."

And, like Ken, he, too, is afraid of what is coming.

Lazarus said that much of the fighting in South Africa is the result of segregation of tribes into townships. "Sutu lived one place. Zulu another. And Xhosa another," he said.

The government dictated not just separation of whites from blacks and coloreds but tribe from tribe.

"If they had been mixed, I don't think fighting would be happening," he said. "But now it is dangerous for a Sutu to go to a Zulu area. People fear Zulus.

"If a Zulu asks to stay in a hostel, then he brings in more. Soon there are a hundred."

*****

I believe, as did Martin Luther King Jr., that a person should be judged by the content of his character and not the color of his skin. But I live in the United States. If I lived in South Africa and had experienced what Ken and so many other whites have, I don't know if I'd believe that. After all, our beliefs are shaped by our experiences.

Tuesday, July 23, Montgomery, Alabama

Well, here I am, gainfully employed again, this time as an assistant editor for B.A.S.S. Publications. After two years of freelance writing, I was hired by Dave Precht, the same man who bought my first magazine article in the spring of 1982 during my first year of teaching.

Oh, yeah, teaching. For eight years, I loved it. Then I crashed and burned. As I jumped up onstage to rehearse my role as master of ceremonies for a school talent show, my heart started racing and wouldn't stop. The doctor said, "You're healthy as a horse, but you have to cut back."

That was the first time I realized I can stress out doing things I enjoy.

I asked the school board for a leave of absence, but it refused. So I quit to freelance.

At the time of my anxiety attack, I was teaching all of the writing-intensive courses, as well as serving as chair of the English Department. I was involved in time-consuming volunteer projects with the kids too, including a holiday charity drive and Project Graduation. I taught a couple of nights a week at the local community college. And I was accumulating more and more magazine assignments, complete with deadlines.

Plus, my social life arguably was the richest it had ever been. I had a great group of friends, both male and female. We played sports, worked out, and partied together. We took trips to fun places like New Orleans.

I loved my life and lived it to the fullest, instead of writing about it.

Now, with it streamlined considerably, I've had time to reflect. I've also had time for other things, like scanning through this journal today when I decided to make an entry. Who knows? Maybe the Africa trip got me going again.

What I noticed most is how many entries I made when I first started teaching in 1981 and how they diminished over the years. I'm guessing that happened because teaching *was* my focus at first. Then, as time passed, it wasn't so much, as I developed relationships and devoted more thought and energy to writing.

Also, I realized how writing in this journal helped me deal with life, especially during the tough times. Maybe I'll get back in the habit again.

Or not. I'm not making any promises. There's this girl down in Sarasota, Lisa, and I'm hoping that she's going to be time-consuming too.

I'm still riding high from the Africa trip. I'll be writing an article for *Bassmaster Magazine* about the fishing part of the adventure.

*****

Dave and Shirley still are on my mind often, but nightmares continue to grow less frequent. I think it helped to talk to Patty Ryan, a features writer for the *Tampa Tribune*, who called recently. Because of Dave and Shirley's prominence in the area and because of the tragic way in which they died, she's doing an in-depth investigative piece.

She told me that most of Dave and Shirley's friends won't talk to her. She said they're mad that they allowed Dave to trick them into giving him money. And they're mad that Dave didn't give Shirley a choice about life or death.

Yeah, I'm mad about that too. But I don't take it personally. They both were my friends. What continues to be so difficult for me is to just accept the fact that they are dead, that I never will see them again—except in my nightmares.

Wednesday, October 2

I received a copy of Patty Ryan's article about Dave and Shirley's murder/suicide today. It was the front-page story in the Bay Life section of the Sunday

Tribune, with a jump to two more pages inside, with lots of photos. She did an extraordinary job of examining their lives and the unique relationship and circumstances that led to the tragedy.

In a note, Patty warned me: "There's a fairly graphic photograph on page five. The story also includes some description of the crime scene, enough to depict how out of character David's actions seemed. I wanted you to be aware of that before you started reading."

Warning me was both the right and kind thing to do. But I looked and read anyway.

That photo showed blood spatters on the wall and a wedding photo eight feet from where Shirley lay dead in their bed.

Along with other less graphic photos, it reminded me of how well I knew their house, just as I knew them, and how often I'd been in those rooms, talking and laughing with them, as well as watching movies, playing games, and eating Shirley's famous chili. I guess seeing the way those rooms looked following the crime should have helped me accept their deaths. But it didn't.

Neither did reading excerpts from Dave's suicide note, which were included in the article:

"I went over the edge and I went crazy. This morning about six, I killed the only person I ever loved."

"I killed Shirley the last two years when I lost all of her money, ruined her business, and ruined her life."

"Even at the end, I wasn't brave enough to tell her the truth because I knew the shame she would feel would devastate her to total collapse."

"Even last night she knew something was wrong with me, but her loved blinded her of my thoughts. I lay awake at three thirty and had a hammer with me, pondering whether I could do this horrible deed."

As it turned out, he could. They're dead. I attended their closed-casket double funeral.

Still, even as this article confirms they are gone, it's so difficult for me to accept, and, with the horror fresh in my mind once again, I'm afraid the nightmares will return with a vengeance.

I must find a way to come to terms with their deaths.

Sunday, December 1

I found a way.

As I drove past Tampa on my way to spend Thanksgiving with Lisa in Sarasota, I realized what I must do. She agreed to help.

From her house, we drove back to Tampa, to the house where Dave and Shirley lived and I visited so often.

Their car was not in the driveway. Someone else's was. The house recently had been painted and was not the color I remember. They were not there. It was not their house anymore. Seeing and realizing those things allowed me to truly grieve for the first time. Yes, I shed a few tears at the funeral, but they were not really enough.

Sitting in the car with Lisa, looking at the house that now belonged to someone else, I cried and cried and cried. I pounded on the steering wheel and yelled at David for being so stupid and for not giving Shirley a choice.

"How could you do this?" I blubbered. "How?

"You had friends."

"We loved you. We could have helped you! You never gave us a chance! I hate you! I hate you! I hate you!"

Then I got out of the car, walked, and cursed and cried for about an hour. After that, Lisa drove us back to Sarasota.

Only time will take away the nightmares for good, I suspect. But I'm definitely better, stronger, and accept that my friends are dead and gone forever.

1992

Tuesday, December 22

More than a year later, this will be my final entry in this journal. A story needs an end, and this is it.

Today I received a Christmas card from Frieda, one of Shirley's friends from St. Louis. Here's what she said in a note that accompanied the card:

"I want you to know I took your advice and went to Tampa. I made my visit to see for myself. I let go of my anger and I reflected. The release was wonderful.

"I still have memories, but I try to remember the good times and the joys we shared together."

As do I.

About the Author

Author Robert U. Montgomery started writing this book more than 40 years ago. Only he didn't know it at the time.

Through journal entries, he shares his experiences as a beginning high school English and journalism teacher in the early 1980s, as he also strived to make his mark as a freelance writer. Because he was not writing for an audience, his entries about those days in the classroom are genuinely candid, sometimes emotional, and often punctuated with humorous insight.

Additionally, he reveals both the joy and the sorrow of his search for companionship and romance, as well as his struggle to deal with family conflict and tragic loss. An adventure in Africa provided welcome relief from the nightmares he suffered because of the latter, as he searched for a way to deal with the senseless and brutal loss of his two best friends.

Montgomery went on to enjoy great success as both an award-winning magazine writer and photographer, before becoming an author. This is his 15th book for both adults and children. Two of them are *Fish, Frogs, and Fireflies: Growing Up with Nature* and *Under the Bed: Tales from an Innocent Childhood*. He also contributed an essay to *Bright Spots: Motivation and Inspiration to Light Your Path in a Changing World*, an international bestseller.

You can learn more about the author and his works at his Amazon Author Page and on Facebook.

He lives in rural Missouri with his dog, Pippa, who co-authored the book *Pippa's Journey: Tail-Wagging Tales of Rescue Dogs*.

www.ingramcontent.com/pod-product-compliance
Lightning Source LLC
Chambersburg PA
CBHW071955070526
44583CB00015B/1207